THE RITUAL GEM OF THE COPTIC CHURCH BETWEEN
THE ORIENTAL AND EASTERN CHURCHES

RITES OF ECCLESIASTICAL FASTS AND FEASTS

THE HOLY PASCHA

LITURGICAL HISTORY & RITES OF THE PRAYERS

BOOK 1

Lazarus Saturday and Palm Sunday

BY

FATHER ATHANASIUS AL-MAKARY

Mary Dawood	*Translator*
Peter Ibrahim	*Editor*
Mena Fawzy Abdelsayed	*Editor-in-Chief*

The Holy Pascha: Liturgical History & Rites of the Prayers
Book 1: Lazarus Saturday and Palm Sunday

The Ritual Gem of the Coptic Church Between the Oriental and Eastern Churches:

Rites of Ecclesiastical Fasts and Feasts

By Father Athanasius al-Makary

Copyright © 2021 by Mena Fawzy Abdelsayed

All rights reserved.

No part of this publication may be reproduced, stored in a retrieval system, or transmitted in any form or by any means—electronic, mechanical, graphic, photocopy, recording, taping, information storage, or any other—without written permission of the copyright owner.

Designed & Published by:
St. Mary & St. Moses Abbey Press
101 S Vista Dr., Sandia, TX 78383
stmabbeypress.com

Introduction to the Rituals of the Coptic Church

This publication was originally available in Arabic in a series of books called *Al-Durra al-Ṭaqsiyya Li-l-Kanīsa al-Qibṭiyya* (The Ritual Gem of the Coptic Church). It outlines the spiritual and deep rituals of the sacraments, feasts and fasts of the Coptic Church in light of the other Oriental and Eastern Churches. This detailed work is found in fifty books in Arabic and focuses on the historical developments of the liturgical life of the Church from the first century onwards based on the writings of the Church Fathers, and the manuscripts and the national and international academic studies of the Coptic liturgy.

TABLE OF CONTENTS

Introduction...viii
   Index of Manuscripts used in this Study...................xii
Part One..1
An Overall View..1
Part Two..30
Lazarus Saturday..30
   Chapter One: The Miracle of Raising Lazarus from the Dead...30
   Chapter Two: The Rites of the Lazarus Saturday Prayers...38
Part Three...58
The Feast of Palm Sunday..58
   Chapter One: About the Feast of Palm Sunday and its Liturgical Observances..58
   Chapter Two: The Rites of Vespers Praise and Raising of Incense Prayers of Palm Sunday..............78
   Chapter Three: The Rite of Praises of Midnight and Lauds on Palm Sunday.......................................113
   Chapter Four: The Rites of Matins Raising of Incense Prayers of Palm Sunday..............................126
   Chapter Five: The Rite of Palm Sunday Liturgy Service..162
   Chapter Six: The Rite of the General Funeral Prayers...203
Bibliography..221

ABBREVIATIONS

BSAC	*Bulletin de la Société d'Archéologie Copte*
CPG	*Clavis Patrum Graecorum*
EH	*Ecclesiastical History*
OCP	*Orientalia Christiana Periodica*
ODCC	*Oxford Distortionary of the Christian Church*
PO	*Patrologia Orientalis*

INTRODUCTION

Strictly speaking, the Great Lent ends with the Friday following the fifth Sunday of the Fast. This period is preceded by a week during which we fast prior to the start of Lent, resulting in a total of forty-seven days of fasting. The Great Lent is then followed by the Fast of Holy Week, that is the week of the Holy Pascha.

St. John Chrysostom (347 – 407 AD) speaks of this Final Week, saying:

> So, just as navigators, runners and prizefighters in each case stretch their enthusiasm and vigilance to the limit at the point when they are close to success, well, in just the same way ought we too, now that we have arrived at this great week, give thanks to God's grace, intensify the devotion of our prayers and give evidence of precise and thorough confession of sins, practice of good works, generous almsgiving, fair dealing, even-tempered behavior and every other virtue, so that we may arrive at the Lord's Day with these good deeds and thus enjoy the Master's generosity.[1]
> (Homily 30, *On Genesis*)

---

[1] John Chrysostom, *On Genesis*, 30, trans. by Robert C. Hill, CUA Press Fathers of the Church Patristic Series 82 (Washington, D.C.: The Catholic University of America Press, 1990), 220.

The book in your hands, dear reader, seeks to trace Jesus' steps during His final days on earth by delving into the Church's rites, prayers, and liturgical worship during these great holy days. These are the days in which we pass from darkness to light, hatred to love, ignorance to enlightenment, being lost to being found, slavery to freedom, despair to hope, perdition to salvation, death to life, and the world's grip to the Fatherly bosom.

The first volume of this book (in Arabic) takes you on a liturgical journey starting with Lazarus Saturday until the end of Wednesday of the Holy Pascha. This is followed by the second volume (in Arabic) which continues the journey until our Lord's entombment at the close of the Good Friday prayers, in anticipation of His Holy Resurrection, which will be the topic of the third volume God-willing.

Kindly note, dear reader, that the treatises and commentaries on the liturgical rituals and ecclesiastical rites presented in this book, are of a purely academic nature. They are meant to explore the history of our liturgy which passed through many stages until we received it as we know it today. An ample number of references were utilized in the composition of this book from the great multitude of manuscripts in both Egyptian and global libraries and museums worldwide. The liturgical studies presented in this book are therefore entirely scholarly and are not intended to change or amend in any way or form any of our liturgical practices or contemporary rites, which is the sole prerogative of the Church hierarchy.

I beseech You, O Holy Father in heaven, through Your beloved Son Jesus Christ, and the intercessions of the Holy Spirit, to enlighten our hearts that, by studying the liturgical prayers, we may discern the deep love by which You loved us which compelled You to offer Your Only Begotten Son on the wood of the Cross for us, through Whom You have redeemed all those who seek You and granted them eternal life through His Holy Resurrection from the dead.

O my Lord and Saviour, Jesus Christ, let this book be as a lit candle before Your holy icon during the week of Your life-giving Passion, for You are the Light that shines on all.

Through the blessings of the intercessions of the ever-virgin Theotokos, the pure St. Mary, and all the heavenly hosts; and the prayers of my masters and fathers the Apostles and the choir of martyrs and saints, and the prayers of his holiness Pope Shenouda III, Pope of Alexandria and Patriarch of the See of St. Mark, and all my fathers the metropolitans, bishops, hegumens and priests, and my brothers the deacons, the monks, and all the blessed laymen. Amen.

Book I: Lazarus Saturday and Palm Sunday

Index of Manuscripts used in this Study

I. **Church Order Manuscripts**
   - Church Order Manuscript No. 118 (Rites) at the Patriarchate in Cairo, transcript dated to 1911.[2] It is referred to in the book as *"Church Order Manuscript No. 118 (Rites) in Cairo Patriarchate 1911."*

   In addition to the following manuscripts:[3]
   - Church Order Manuscript at the library of the Patriarchate in Cairo, transcript dated to 1160 AM / 1444 AD. It is referred to in the book as *"Church Order Manuscript No. 73 (Rites) in Cairo Patriarchate for the year 1444."*
   - Church Order Manuscript at the library of Al-Baramūs Monastery, transcript dated to 1230 AM / 1514 AD. It is referred to in the book as *"Manuscript of Al-Baramūs Monastery 1514."*
   - Church Order Manuscript at the library of St. Antony Monastery, transcript dated to 1377 AM / 1661 AD. It is referred to in the book as *"Manuscript of St. Antony Monastery 1661."*

---

[2] Facsimile.

[3] These manuscripts are not numbered. The quotes are taken from the book by Samuel of Shibīn Al-Qanater, *The Church Order as per the Patriarchate manuscripts in Cairo and Alexandria and the manuscripts of the monasteries and churches*, Volume 3 (Cairo: 2000).

- Church Order Manuscript at the library of the Syrian Monastery, transcript dated to 1414 AM / 1698 AD. It is referred to in the book as *"Manuscript of the Syrian Monastery 1698."*
- Church Order Manuscript at the library of the Syrian Monastery, transcript dated to 1435 AM / 1719 AD. It is referred to in the book as *"Manuscript of the Syrian Monastery 1719."*
- Church Order Manuscript at the library of the Patriarchate in Alexandria, transcript dated to 1432 AM / 1716 AD.[4] It is referred to in the book as *"Manuscript of Alexandria Patriarchate 1716."*

II. **Manuscripts of the Book, *The Lamp that Lights in the Darkness In Clarifying the Service (Miṣbāḥ al-ẓulma wa 'īdāḥ al-khidma)***
- Reference is made to what Shams Al-Riʾāsa Abū Al-Barakāt Ibn Kabar (1324 AD) mentions in Chapter 18[5] of his book, *The Lamp that Lights in the Darkness In Clarifying the Service (Miṣbāḥ al-ẓulma wa 'īdāḥ al-khidma)*, as transcribed in two main manuscripts:

---

[4] This manuscript is critical as it includes the rites and prayers practiced in the churches of Old Cairo, as evidenced in the manuscript itself.

[5] This chapter is dedicated to the order of the Great Lent, Palm Sunday, Paschal Weekdays, Maundy Thursday, Good Friday, Bright Saturday, Resurrection Sunday, and the order of the Pascha in St. Makarios Monastery.

- Manuscript No. 203 (Arabic) at the National Library of Paris, transcript dated to the Papacy of Abba Yo'annis X, the 85th Patriarch of Alexandria (1363 – 1369 AD).

Chapter 18 covers the pages 208 (front) – 211 (back) and 220 (front), while the eight pages of 212 (front) – 219 (back) are missing from the manuscript. That is, only four and half pages remain from Chapter 18 of this manuscript in Paris, which is an unfortunate and irreversible loss to the literature.

I was alarmed by this academic misfortune during my studies of the rites of the Holy Pascha Week prayers, especially those of Maundy Thursday which are missing from the manuscript in Paris. I contacted the library of Uppsala University in Sweden to obtain a photocopy of Chapter 18 of the book, *The Lamp that Lights in the Darkness In Clarifying the Service (Miṣbāḥ al-ẓulma wa 'īdāḥ al-khidma)*, that is kept there, whose transcript (Vet. 12) is older than that of the one in Paris.

Afterwards, I learned that Chapter 18 from the Uppsala manuscripts was verified and published in 2001 by Wadi, the Franciscan brother, in volume (collection) No. 34 of the publications of the Franciscan Centre of Christian Oriental Studies.[6] Upon procuring a copy of this document, I found the following comment on these eight missing pages:

> ... The loss of these pages is an immeasurable loss to the literature, especially that this manuscript is the oldest, and in some aspect presents a different order to that found in other manuscripts. Among all the manuscripts we found, none has a definite direct quotation from this manuscript.[7]

This manuscript is referred to in the book as the *"Manuscript of Paris."*

- Manuscript No. (Vet. 12) at the Library of Uppsala, Sweden. It is dated back to 4 Meshir 1263 AM / 1546 AD, which is a transcript copied from the original transcript dated 27 Paremhat 1073 AM / 1357 AD. Thus, the original transcript is a little older than the *Manuscript of Paris* and

---

[6] *Studia Orientalia Christiana, Collectanea 34, Studia – Documenta,* (Cairo – Jerusalem: The Franciscan Center of Christian Oriental Studies, 2001).

[7] Wadi the Franciscan, *Christian Oriental Studies*, Volume 34 (Cairo – Jerusalem: The Franciscan Center of Christian Oriental Studies, 2001), 244.

The advantage of the Parisian manuscript is that the hands of transcribers did not trifle with it, since the date of its transcript is less than 25 years after the departure of Ibn Kabar. In addition, it is customary for scribes while transcribing an old manuscript to add the new liturgical practices of their own age or to take off the forfeited ones.

renders a different redaction in several cases. Furthermore, the scribe declares on page 258 (front) that he omitted specific sections, among which is the missing text in Chapter 18[8] regarding the ordo of the Olive Procession on Palm Sunday.

This manuscript is referred to in the book as the *"Manuscript of Uppsala."* The time lapse between the *Manuscript of Paris* and the *Manuscript of Uppsala* is about 177 years, which is not a short period.

A third manuscript of the book, *The Lamp that Lights in the Darkness In Clarifying the Service (Miṣbāḥ al-ẓulma wa 'īdāḥ al-khidma)*, exists in the Vatican library, coded as No. 623 (Arabic). This manuscript is not dated but is thought to be a copy of the Uppsala Manuscript which dates to the sixteenth century. The Coptic texts are mostly written in the left column, regardless of their position in the sentence which may have thus been added by a later scribe in this manner due to the lack of space. Furthermore, in several cases, the scribe leaves the sentence incomplete more

---

[8] Wadi the Franciscan, *Christian Oriental Studies*, Volume 34, *op. cit.*, 244-245.

often compared to the text of the Uppsala Manuscript.⁹

Since this manuscript appears to be a copy of the Uppsala Manuscript, as I have noticed myself, I will only refer to it in case it includes core differences from the former.

There is another manuscript kept in the Coptic Museum, which is coded No. 375 (Theology) and dates to 1932/1933 AD. This is in addition to the second half of the Manuscript of Shenouda Al-Baramūsī, which dates to 1955 AD.¹⁰ Both manuscripts include the text that the Uppsala and Vatican Manuscripts omitted, yet in a different location than that stated in the Paris Manuscript.¹¹

The first attempt to publish Chapter 18 of the book, *The Lamp that Lights in the Darkness In Clarifying the Service (Miṣbāḥ al-ẓulma wa 'īdāḥ al-khidma)*, was made by George Philotheos 'Awaḍ, who used it as an introduction to the Pascha Book

---

⁹ Wadi the Franciscan, *op. cit.*, 245.
¹⁰ Edited for publishing by Fr. Samuel Al-Soriānī (Bishop Samuel of Shibīn Al-Qanater) (Cairo: 1992). Although there is no mention that this edition is a copy of the transcript of Shenouda Al-Baramūsī, his name is mentioned as a transcriber in page 316.
¹¹ Wadi the Franciscan, *Christian Oriental Studies*, Volume 34, *op. cit.*, 245-246.

that Fr Bakhūm Al-Baramūsī intended to print. However, this book appeared in Alexandria in 1921 without this introduction. George Philotheos 'Awaḍ affirmed it was Pope Cyril V (1874 – 1927) who ordered the exclusion of this introduction from the printed book.[12]

III. Manuscripts of the Order of the Passion Week

- Copto-Arabic Manuscript No. 32 (Coptic) at the National Library of Paris (a copy). The transcript dates to Wednesday, 1 Thout 1226 AM / 29 August 1509 AD. This manuscript describes the rites practiced during the fifteenth century covering several historical and liturgical topics. What concerns us from it is the demonstration of the order of the Friday of the Holy Pascha according to the rites practiced in St. Mary Church in the Roman Quarter of Old Cairo. Specifically, we will focus on the part titled "The Order of Good Friday, the Friday of Salvation, in the Roman Quarter."[13] It is referred to in this book as *"Manuscript of the Roman Quarter Typikon (5th century)."*

---

[12] Wadi the Franciscan, *Christian Oriental Studies*, Volume 34, *op. cit.*, 243.

[13] About this manuscript, refer to Majid Ṣobḥī Rizk, Journal of New Vine (2008), 205.

- Copto-Arabic Manuscript No. 36 (Coptic) at the National Library of Paris (a copy). The first line of the manuscript reads:

  > With the help and good felicitation of the Almighty God, we begin the order of Friday of the life-giving Passion of our Lord Jesus Christ, to whom is all glory.

  The other side of the manuscript presents (as if it were an Arabic book) the complete text of the book "The Mystery of the Trinity in the Service of Priesthood."[14] However, I was unable to ascertain the location or date of the copy of this manuscript. It is referred to in this book as *"The Manuscript of the Parisian Typikon."*

- Copto-Arabic Manuscript No. 31 (Coptic) at the Library of the Coptic Museum in Old Cairo (a copy). The first lines of the manuscript read:

  > In the name of the merciful and companionate God. A permanent and everlasting estate of the Church of the great saint Abba Shenoute in Darb Al-Tangīr.[15] It cannot be sold or rented out. Whoever takes it and returns it shall be absolved and blessed. Whoever takes it and does not return

---

[14] I have referred to and quoted from this important book in the *Divine Liturgy: The Mystery of the Kingdom of God.*

[15] I was unable to read the work in the manuscript, and so I drew it. The place is in Old Cairo.

it shall be under the condemnation of the Cross and have a share with Simon the Sorcerer, Diocletian the Infidel, and Judas Iscariot.

It dates to the fourteenth century, around the time of Fr Abū Al-Barakāt Ibn Kabar, making it an extremely significant manuscript. It represents the rites of Pascha in one of the churches of Old Cairo. It is referred to in this book as *"The Manuscript of Abba Shenoute Typikon (14th century)."*

- Copto-Arabic Manuscript No. 336 (Rites) at the library of the Coptic Museum in Old Cairo (a copy). It demonstrates the order of Pascha Friday according to the rites of St. Mary's Hanging Church in Old Cairo. The first lines of the manuscript read:

    > In the name of God. The order of the live-giving Passion Friday as practiced in the Hanging Church of our Lady.

    The end of the manuscript evinces that it was transcribed during the Papacy of Pope Gabriel VII (1525 – 2568), the 95th Patriarch of the Coptic Church. It is referred to in this book as *"The Manuscript of the Hanging Church Typikon (16th century)."*

Book I: Lazarus Saturday and Palm Sunday

- Copto-Arabic Manuscript No. 184 (Rites) at the Library of the Coptic Museum in Old Cairo. It represents the order of Friday of the Holy Pascha according to the rites of St. Mary's Hanging Church in Old Cairo. The first lines of the manuscript read:

> In the name of God. With the help and good felicitation of God, we begin transcribing the book of Friday of the life-giving Passion as observed in the Hanging Church of our Lady.

After relating the rites of Lazarus Saturday and Palm Sunday, we read on page 34 (recto) the following:

> This concludes the order of Lazarus Saturday and Palm Sunday. Remember, O Lord, your poor and sinful servant the transcriber, Nesīm Ibn Abū ..., who beseeches every reader to ask for the forgiveness of his sins.

The manuscript continues in page 34 (verso):

> A permanent and everlasting estate of St. George Church, known as the Ethiopian Church in Hāret Zuweila, the Upper Church next to the Armenian Church. Reward, O Lord, the dear brother, Man Al-Hariri, the honourable deacon who oversees the holy Church... May God bless him. With the blessing of the great martyr St. George, may God reward him with the incorruptible instead of the

> corruptible, the heavenly[16] instead of the earthly... etc.

The end of the manuscript reads:

> The one who oversaw this work is the blessed scribe and dear brother Manqūriūs Al-Harīrī, the honourable deacon and overseer of the Church...[17]

The date of transcription is written at the beginning of the manuscript in modern handwriting as the 16th C (i.e., century) 1672 AD. It is referred to in this book as *"The Manuscript of the Haret Zuweila Typikon (17th century)."*

- Copto-Arabic Manuscript No. 51 (Rites) at the library of the Coptic Museum in Old Cairo (a copy). It represents the order of Holy Pascha Friday according to the rites of St. Mary's Hanging Church. The first lines of the manuscript read:

> In the name of God. The order of Friday of the life-giving Passion as practiced in the Hanging Church of our Lady.

Despite being defaced towards the end, this manuscript is useful in comparing the text with

---

[16] In the manuscript, it is "heavenly."
[17] Henceforth the writings are completely defaced and unreadable.

the two aforementioned manuscripts. It is referred to in this book as *"The Manuscript of the Hanging Church Typikon."*

- Copto-Arabic Manuscript No. 8770 (Oriental) at the British Library in London (a copy). The first lines of the manuscript read:

    > In the name of the Almighty God. With the help of our Lord Jesus Christ, we begin the order of Friday of the Passion in the peace of God. Amen.

    Both the Coptic and the Arabic handwriting are not legible, and some parts are defaced, especially towards the end. It was neither possible to determine the date of its transcription or the church it belonged to. However, from the form of the handwriting, it may be possible to date it to the eighteenth or nineteenth century. It is referred to in this book as *"The Manuscript of the London Typikon."*

IV. **Manuscripts of the Holy Paschal Week Lectionary**
- Arabic Manuscript No. 260 (Rites) at the Library of St. Antony Monastery in the Eastern Desert. A colophon at the beginning of the manuscript

shows a priest from this monastery transcribed it. The first lines of the manuscript read:[18]

> In the name of the Holy Trinity, One God. With the help of our Lord Jesus Christ, we begin to transcribe the prayers of the evening and morning hours of the holy Paschal Week.

The end of the manuscript reads:[19]

> In the name of the merciful and compassionate God. A permanent and everlasting estate of the church of St. Antony Monastery in Al-Qalzam Mountain. It cannot be sold, rented out, or owned by any priest or monk. It cannot be kept in any monk's cell, or leave the monastery unless absolutely necessary … The son of obedience shall receive blessing. Thanks be to God forever.

The colophon containing the manuscript's transcription date is also mentioned at the end but is barely legible: "First of Pharmuthi 900 AM." This is the same date used by the monks when creating an index for the monastery's manuscripts.[20] Accordingly, this lectionary traces back to the year 1184 AD, that is, the end of the twelfth century. Hence, it is considered one of the oldest lectionaries of the Paschal Week that are

---

[18] After correcting the linguistic and grammatical errors.
[19] After correcting the linguistic and grammatical errors.
[20] A blessed effort that is due praise and gratitude.

known to date. I have verified this myself. It is referred to in this book as *"The Manuscript of St. Antony Lectionary (12th century)."*

- Copto-Arabic Lectionary Manuscript No. 5997 (Appendices), a copy. The colophon at the end of the manuscript reads:

  > With the help of God, we conclude what is read during the Holy Paschal Week from its first day until the end of Resurrection Sunday on which Christ, the Son of God and our King and Saviour truly rose on the twenty-second of Thout in the year 909 AM.[21] Remember, O Lord, your servant, Ⲑⲱⲙ(ⲁ)ⲥ.

  It is referred to in this book as *"Manuscript of London Lectionary (12th century)."*

- Copto-Arabic Lectionary Manuscript No. 70 (Coptic) at the National Library of Paris. The first lines of the manuscript read:

  > With the help of God, we begin to transcribe what is read over the six days of the Passover of our salvation. Amen.

---

[21] Which corresponds to the year 1192 AD.

O.H.E. Burmester verifies that it goes back to the year 1319 AD.[22] It is referred to in this book as *"Manuscript of Paris Lectionary (14th century)."*

Note:
To allow this book to be of a sensible size, dear reader, I will not refer to all the aforementioned manuscripts in every liturgical element, except when core differences exist that would support and enrich the study.

It is important for the dear reader to make the distinction between the term "manuscripts under study," which refers to items I, II and III, and the term "lectionary manuscripts under study," which refers to item VI.

---

[22] Oswald H.E. KHS-Burmester, *Le lectionaire copte de la semain sainte*, PO, t.24, fas.2 (Paris: Firmin-Didot, 1933), 173, 174, 176.

Part One

An Overall View

Between "Pascha" and "Passover"
The word "Pascha"[1] is Aramaic, which is informal (slang) Hebrew. It was transliterated with the same pronunciation in the Greek and Arabic languages as πάσχα, as well as many European languages, and it means "Passover." The word bears no relation to the notions of "suffering" or "passion." In Greek, the word for pain is πάσχω (páskhō), which is distinct from the word "Pascha." The Latin word "passio" which means "suffering" possibly contributed to the conflation of these two meanings.

Another Aramaic word is "Fṣḥā," from which the Arabic word "Fiṣḥ" is derived, which also means "Passover." This refers to when the Angel of death

---

[1] I would like to point out that this word is often written as "Passcha" in the manuscripts. However, I will make the writing consistent throughout the book in your hands, as well as in the footnotes.

passed over the houses marked with the blood of the Paschal lamb.[2] The New Testament uses this term to refer to the Jewish Feast of Passover and the Feast of Resurrection in the Christian Church. The term is also used to refer to the "Eucharistic Table" and the "Second Coming of the Lord" which is called the "Lord's Passover."

In the early Church, the word "Pascha" was used to refer to the annual commemoration of the Lord's death and resurrection, that is to both Good Friday and the Feast of the Resurrection.[3] On the other hand, St. Irenaeus (130 – 200 AD) and Tertullian the Scholar (160 – 225 AD) used the word "Pascha" to refer to Good Friday only. The latter practice can also be found in the book of the *Apostolic Tradition*, written before 235 AD, in which Chapter 29 is titled "The Passover Fast." This chapter deals with the fast of Pascha, which, at that time, was limited to Friday and Saturday. When the *Apostolic Tradition* speaks of the Day of "Pascha," it refers to Bright Saturday. Fasting the two days before the Resurrection was well known in the early Church and is considered the oldest fast known to the universal church. Here, the book of the *Apostolic Tradition* does not differentiate between the terms "Passover" and "Pascha."

---

[2] Exodus 12:13
[3] *ODCC*, 2nd edition, 1039.

With respect to the Church of Alexandria, we find that the Paschal Letters of Pope Athanasius the Apostolic (328 – 373 AD) speak of the "Passover Week," which refers to the fasting of the six days preceding the Feast of the Resurrection. For example, the second Paschal Letter reads:

> … After we have given ourselves to fasting in continued succession, let us begin the holy Passover week.

After the time of Pope Athanasius the Apostolic, the title of this week in Egypt was known exclusively as the "Paschal Week." In Canon No. 57 of Pope Athanasius, the Patriarch of Alexandria, which was written near the end of the fifth century, we find the term "the holy Paschal week."[4] Furthermore, the Apostolic Coptic Canons, which were written around the same time, solely refer to the week as the "Paschal week." We can find the same pattern in the Heliopolis Coptic Canons, which were written during the sixth century, as well as the Egyptian Canons of St. Basil the Great written

---

[4] The expression "holy Paschal week" did not appear in the letters of Pope Athanasius the Apostolic, who actually referred to this week as the "Passover week." This is further evidence that these canons were not decreed by Pope Athanasius the Apostolic, but rather by Pope Athanasius II (489 – 496 AD), the 27th Patriarch, who is known in the Church as Athanasius the Little to distinguish him from Athanasius the Great, the 20th Patriarch. For further details refer to my book "The Canons of Pope Athanasius II."

during the aforementioned period[5], during which we, again find the terms "Pascha" and the "Great Pascha" used.

The book of the *Apostolic Tradition* by Hippolytus, written before 235 AD, is one of the earliest extant references speaking of "Pascha," as previously pointed out, even prior to the term "Paschal Week." On the other hand, one of the earliest references using the expression "Paschal Week" is the collection of the *Apostolic Constitutions* books, written in the fourth century. Among these, the book *Didascalia/Didache*, meaning the *Teachings of the Apostles* was translated into Arabic and was widely circulated throughout the East. This same expression is also found in the canons of the Council of Carthage (345 – 348 AD), known as the Canons of the African Church.

Thus, it appears that over the years, the term "Passover Week," the earlier expression known in the Church of Alexandria nearly disappeared and the term "Paschal Week" replaced it, while the expression of the "Final Week" is considered the oldest title for the holy Paschal Week.

Therefore, using the term "Paschal Week" or "Passover Week" in our context here is linguistically the same, for

---

[5] For further clarification of this point, kindly refer to my book "The Egyptianizing of Canons attributed to Basil the Great."

the word "Pascha" refers to the Jewish Feast of Passover as well as to the Christian Passover Week, that is the week that precedes the Feast of Resurrection, as previously pointed out.

When I said that "the term Passover Week has **almost** disappeared," I meant that it has not entirely vanished but that it is much less used. Hence, we read in the tenth century the expression "Paschal Week, that is the Passover Week"[6] by Anba Severus Ibn Al-Muqaffaʿ (departed 987 AD).

About the Term "Passion Week"
The term "Passion Week" is more prevalent today among the Copts, although it is not an accurate label. In fact, it is an incorrect term because the sufferings Christ suffered are not ordinary; rather, they are saving and life-giving passions. The word "passion" means nothing more than pain and suffering, while the saving and life-giving passion refers to the Passion of our Lord for us that became the means for our resurrection and life. Hence, Christ transformed the idea of pain from punishment and a curse to a divine gift which bestows life and glory to those who undergo it.

---

[6] Severus Ibn Al-Muqaffaʿ of Al-Ashmūnīn, *The Precious Pearls in Explaining the Faith* (Tosson, Shubra: Archangel Michael Church, 1987), 180.

In the late seventh century, the expression "Salutatory Passion Week" appeared, which is the term used in Canon 89 of the Council of Trullo (692). It is important for the reader to note that the term "Passion Week" or "Passion Friday" has neither appeared in any writings or canon laws of the Alexandrian fathers nor in the canons of the Coptic Patriarchs in the Middle Ages. The term used in the Coptic Church in the Middle Ages was "Paschal Friday." The Church Ordo manuscripts, which continued to be written until the beginning of the twentieth century, always read "The Order of Friday of the Life-Giving Passion."[7] Yoḥanna Ibn Sebā', in the thirteenth century, is the only one who mentions the term "Friday of the Passion," saying:

> ... the reason for conducting a funeral for them during this time is that **Passion Friday** is reserved for Christ's Passion ...[8]

---

[7] Unfortunately, when the Lectionary of the holy Paschal week was printed, it was called "The Passion Week Lectionary." The printing presses hastily overlooked our ancient tradition that we kept in writing verbatim with the aid of the lights of candles and kerosene lamps.

[8] Yoḥanna Ibn Zakaria Ibn Sebā', *Book of the Precious Jewel in Church Sciences (Ketāb al-Jawhara al-Nafīsa Fī 'Oloum al-Kanīsa)*, ver. and trans. to Latin by Father Victor Mansour Mestarīḥ the Franciscan (Cairo: The Franciscan Center for Eastern Christian Studies, 1966), 323.

He also mentions the terms "Christian Passion Friday"[9] and "Passion Hymns."[10] However, when he refers to the book used in the prayers of this final week, he calls it the "Paschal Book."[11]

Over the years, however, the term "Passion Week" became more prevalent among Copts than any of the other labels. The Russian Church is also using this term, while the Greek Church calls it the "Great Holy Week," and the Latins call it the "Great Week" or "Holy Week." Yet, the Latins use the expression "Passion Week" to refer to the week preceding Palm Sunday, which is referred to by the Greeks as "Palm Week."[12]

This is a comprehensive overview of the labels for the final week of the Great Lent over the years.

The Church of Jerusalem is the first to celebrate this Great Week

The events of the final days of our Saviour's life on earth have been the centre of the Church's attention since the beginning, especially in the Eastern Church. The Church of Jerusalem is the first to celebrate this Holy Week, as portrayed by the diary of the fourth-century Spanish

---

[9] *Ibid.*, 324.
[10] *Ibid.*, 329.
[11] *Ibid.*, 325.
[12] *Know Your Church*, Series 12 (The Light Publications, 1983), 115.

pilgrim, Egeria, in 388 AD. Both East and West have since adopted its observance.

In Jerusalem, the celebration of the Great Holy Week started on Saturday, the eve of Palm Sunday, with a liturgical service held in the church called the *Lazarium* in Bethany. On Palm Sunday, they would lead a great procession to the Mount of Olives, and from there to the city of Jerusalem, carrying palms and olive branches in their hands. On Tuesday, they would return to the Mount of Olives, where the presbyters read Christ's prophecy about the destruction of Jerusalem and the end of days.[13] On Wednesday, they read the parts about Judas' betrayal at the holy tomb.[14]

Then, they spent Thursday night until Friday morning on the Mount of Olives in Gethsemane.[15] On Friday morning, they commemorated Jesus' trial before Pilate,[16] and at noon, they brought out the wood of the Holy Cross, which Queen Helen had found, and read pericopes about Jesus' passion, along with Old Testament prophecies, for approximately three hours. Some would spend the entire night in vigil. There is no service on Saturday morning, but all churches would

---

[13] Mark 5:13-37.
[14] Mark 14:10-11.
[15] Mark 14:32-52.
[16] Mark 15:2-15.

fast in commemoration of the Bridegroom's absence.[17] The paramount period of celebration lies from Saturday night until Sunday morning, which was considered to be the mother of all holy vigils, during which the whole world stays awake[18] and spent the entire night in prayer, readings, and praises.

In agreement with the diary of the Spanish pilgrim, Egeria, we read in the *Syrian Didascalia* from the third century:

> You shall convene, watch, and keep vigil throughout the whole night with prayers and intercessions, with readings from the prophets and the Gospel together with psalms. You will do so with fear and great reverence and with diligent supplication until the third hour of the night after Saturday... Then offer your sacrifices; thereafter eat and be of good cheer, rejoice, and be glad because Christ, the pledge of our resurrection, has risen (5:19).[19]

Eusebius of Caesarea (260 – 340 AD) mentions in his book "Life of Constantine" (1:4:18) about this great Holy Week that, after the First Ecumenical Council of Nicaea in 325 AD, Emperor Constantine had ordered these days to be observed with great diligence; and that due to this imperial order the celebration became even more

---

[17] Mark 2:20.
[18] Refer to Homily 219 of St. Augustine.
[19] *Our Liturgical Life*, 1st-year (1989-1990), 445-446.

important and more widespread. Sozomen the historian also confirms this fact in the early fifth century.[20]

The Beginning of Fasting the Holy Paschal Week in the Coptic Tradition

The earlies stages of fasting Holy Week can be found from the mid-third century in Egypt from a letter sent by Pope Dionysius the Great (248 – 265 AD) to Basil, Bishop of Pentapolis.[21] This letter is considered the first ecclesiastical document on the fasting in the Catholic Church. In this letter, Pope Dionisius wrote:

> ... For all do not continue during the six days of the fast either equally or similarly: but some remain without food until cockcrow on all the days, some on two, or three, or four, and some on none of them... some, so far from prolonging their fast do not fast at all, but feed luxuriously during the earlier days of the week, and then, when they come to the last two and prolong their fast on them alone, viz. on Friday and Saturday, think they are performing some great feat by continuing until dawn, I do not hold that they have exercised an equal discipline with those who have practised it for longer periods.

---

[20] Sozomen, *EH*, 1.8.
[21] Pope Dionysius wrote him many letters, of which only this one (1569 *CPG*) remains to date. It became a firm piece of law in the Universal Church. Refer to my book, *Index for Writings of Fathers of the Church of Alexandria – Greek Writings*, 159 (Arabic).

Thus, we can see that, in the beginning, there was much divergence in the traditions of the different churches regarding the feast of the Paschal Week. But soon afterwards, the fast of the six days was settled throughout the Catholic Church.

The *Didascalia* (end of the third century) mentions the six-day fast of the Great Week in the Antiochene Rite.

Soon the six-day fast became fixed in the Alexandrian tradition as well, which can be clearly seen in the first paschal letter of Pope Athanasius the Apostolic of 329 AD. In this letter he calls the Paschal or Passover Week "the holy fast," because that year was the last to have the forty-day fast of the Great Lent separate from the fast of the Paschal Week.[22] Pope Athanasius the Apostolic writes:

> We begin the holy fast on the fifth day of Pharmuthi (March 31) and add to it, according to the number, those six holy and great days which are the symbol of the creation of this world. Let us rest and cease (from fasting) on the tenth day of the

---

[22] This point is explained in detail in my book, *The Fast of Nineveh and the Great Holy Lent*, where I prove that the fast of the holy forty days was merged to the fast of the holy Paschal Week in the year 330 AD in the days of Pope Athanasius the Apostolic, and not in the days of Pope Demetrius the Vinedresser (189 – 231 AD) as written in the Synaxarion of the Coptic Church, which quotes Ibn Kabar (1324 AD).

same Pharmuthi (April 5), on the holy Sabbath of the week.

Thus, in Egypt in the year 329 AD, the fast of the Paschal or Passover Week began on Monday, March 31st with Good Friday celebrated on April 4th that year, and Bright Saturday on April 5th.

Furthermore, in his second paschal letter of the year 330 AD, we find that the Monday of Pascha was the 18th of Pharmuthi (13 April), of which Pope Athanasius the Apostolic says:

> … let us begin the holy Paschal week.

The same pattern can be found in the rest of his paschal letters. Likewise, the paschal letters of St. Cyril the Great confirm that the Paschal Week was six days from Monday to Bright Saturday.

The same is also cited by Ibn Sebā' and Ibn Kabar in the thirteenth and fourteenth centuries. In the thirteenth century, we find Ibn Sebā' writing: "Pascha starts on the eleventh hour of Sunday"[23], that is Palm Sunday, and continues to say: "At the time of sunset on that Sunday, they commence the Christian Passion Week."[24] Concerning Palm Sunday, we find Ibn Kabar (1324 AD)

---

[23] Yoḥanna Ibn Zakaria Ibn Sebā', *op. cit.*, 324.
[24] *Ibid.*, 324.

writing: "From the vigil of that Sunday the statuses of the Passion Week are set in place," that is the evening of Palm Sunday.

However, it is important to note that a key tenth century text indicates that the Holy Paschal Week began on Lazarus Saturday, and not the Paschal Monday. This document was written by Anba Severus Ibn Al-Muqaffa' (departed in 987 AD), Bishop of Al-Ashmūnīn, where he mentions that Lazarus Saturday is to be counted with the Paschal Week for a particular purpose, which he explains later on. He says, and I quote:

> The last week, that is the Paschal Week, is not part of the Great Lent. Rather, we fast that week to commemorate the Passion of our Saviour. We observe it from Lazarus Saturday until Bright Saturday. Accordingly, the forty days, which our Lord fasted for us[25], begin on Monday of the second week[26] and end on the morning of Lazarus Saturday of the seventh week... from the morning of Saturday, that is Lazarus Saturday, we begin to fast in commemoration of the passion and sufferings of our Saviour for us... until the vigil of Bright Saturday.[27]

---

[25] When we say: "Christ suffered for us," we do not mean that He "suffered instead of us," but that He "suffered for our sakes."
[26] Here, he does not count the first week, known as "Heraclius week," of "preparation week," in the forty days of the Great Lent.
[27] That is, till the conclusion of the prayers of Good Friday, which extend till the end of the day. Refer to: Severus Ibn Al-Muqaffa' of Al-Ashmūnīn, *The Precious Pearls in Explaining the Faith, op. cit.*, 181.

Anba Severus Ibn Al-Muqaffa' continues to explain this by saying:

> The Greeks and people of Constantinople, which we call the Armenians –as opposed to the Romans who are the people of Rome, start fasting from the second week, which is the beginning of the forty days of the Great Lent. They do not fast the Heraclius week. Thus, they all start fasting from the beginning of the forty days, and they conclude their fasting in the morning of Lazarus Saturday until the vigil of Bright Saturday. The Romans, on the other hand, do not fast the Monday and Tuesday in which the Greeks, the Armenians and the Syrians start fasting. Instead, they begin fasting on Wednesday, making the end of the forty days of the Great Lent on Palm Sunday. From Paschal Monday they then begin fasting in commemoration of our Saviour's passions, believing that the fast of our Saviour's Passion should commence on Monday and not Lazarus Saturday. Everyone agrees on the latter, but I wanted to show you that Saturday and Sunday are part of the forty days of the Great Lent, in which we should abstain from all passions like the other days of the Great Lent, for we ought to fast for forty consecutive days, day and night...[28]

What Anba Severus Ibn Al-Muqaffa' points out here should not be overlooked. According to him, the Paschal Week starts on Lazarus Saturday, and not Paschal Monday. This is the same rite practiced by the Jerusalem

---

[28] *Ibid.*, 182.

Church Jerusalem, in which Palm Sunday is counted as part of the holy Paschal Week.[29]

Hence, we can see that, in the first five centuries and slightly after, specifically in the days of Pope Athanasius the Apostolic, the fast of the holy six days began on the Monday, and this was distinct and separate from the Great Lent until the time of Pope Athanasius the Apostolic (328 - 373 AD), who merged both fasts together in the year 330 AD. After prepending the Great Lent to the fast of the six days, the start of the latter commenced on the Paschal Monday, while the status of fasting the Saturday and Sunday following the Last Friday of the Great Lent was ambiguous during this early stage. That is, during these times, Lazarus Saturday and Palm Sunday were counted outside of both fasts.

The subsequent development is clearly noticed in the tenth century from the writings of Anba Severus Ibn Al-Muqaffa', although I believe it began a few centuries prior. Through this development, Coptic tradition reverted to following the Jerusalem rite in which the holy Paschal Week commenced on Lazarus Saturday, thus including Palm Sunday as part of the Paschal Week. In other words, the writings of Anba Severus Ibn Al-Muqaffa' in the tenth century documented a rite that

---

[29] Dom Emmanuel Lanne, "Textes et rites de la liturgie pascale dans l'ancienne église Copte," *L'Orient Syrien 6* (1961), 287.

was already practiced in the Church a few centuries prior.

The most astonishing peculiarity, however, is that, beginning from the thirteenth century onwards, Coptic tradition once more considered Monday to be the start of the holy Paschal Week.

How did this happen? Why did the ancient Coptic references revert back to what other surrounding Eastern Churches, like the Byzantine Church for example, affirm about the start of the holy Paschal Week, especially given Anba Severus Ibn Al-Muqaffa's great influence as a renowned scholar and honoured bishop in the Coptic Church whose many writings attest to his ingenuity? Undoubtedly, the reversion to beginning the Paschal Week on the Monday instead of the Saturday prior must be due to the influence of a pivotal liturgical event or a prominent rite of one of the notable bishops or Patriarchs of the Coptic Church who succeeded the time of Anba Severus Ibn Al-Muqaffa' (d. 987 AD).

The rite of the General Funeral Prayer was this new and pivotal liturgical event, which follows the Palm Sunday Liturgy. This rite is practiced only in the Church of Egypt and does not exist elsewhere in the world.

Therefore, I will defer the discussion of this matter to the section discussing the rite of the General Funeral Prayer following the Palm Sunday liturgy.

Features of the Holy Paschal Week in the Coptic Church

The Coptic Church greatly reveres the holy days of Pascha, giving them a unique and privileged status, to the extent that they override the celebration of the Feast of Annunciation, the first Lordly feast in the Catholic Church, if falling between the Last Friday of the Great Lent and the second day of the Feast of the Resurrection. On the other hand, the Byzantine Typikon provides fifteen different alternatives for celebrating the Annunciation Feast, including the possibility of falling during the final three days of the holy Paschal Week. It even allows for and advocates praying the divine liturgy on the morning of Good Friday, although it is generally a day during which the Eucharist sacrifice ought not to be offered. However, the Byzantine Church later rectified this practice. We read in the Arabic version of the Typikon, published in Egypt in 1899 and carefully translated by Archimandrite Gerasimos Mesarra, Metropolitan of Beirut, the following passage regarding the Feast of the Annunciation:

> If the feast of the Annunciation falls on Holy Friday or Saturday, the celebration is pushed to Passover Sunday, and its service chanted alongside that of the Resurrection.

This transfer has been established for just over a century [i.e., in the late eighteenth century] specifically for churches of the cities and villages, in order to avoid any confusion that mingling joyful and funeral tunes might cause to the congregation's ears. As for the monasteries, they are free to keep the order they were instituted on out of respect to the founders of their communities, that is to chant both services together or in accordance with whenever it falls.

It is important to note here that in the Eastern Orthodox Churches, which use the revised Julian calendar, the Feast of Annunciation never falls after Maundy Thursday. As for churches still using the Julian calendar for all their feasts, the Feast of Annunciation could still fall on Good Friday up to the Tuesday of the week following Pascha.

On the evening of Palm Sunday, the church is adorned with sombre decorations of sorrow. The altar is left uncovered until the morning of Maundy Thursday. Likewise, the floor of the sanctuary is uncovered, and its door remains shut and covered with black cloth. The first chorus is left, its lights remain turned off, and the prayers are offered outside of both as a symbol of Christ who was sacrificed on the Cross outside the walls of Jerusalem[30]. The icon of the crucifix or the crown of thorns is placed in the heart of the church nave outside the first choir, with lit candles placed in front of it. When entering the church, one prostrates before the icon of the

---

[30] Hebrews 13:12-13

life-giving passion. Two lecterns are placed on the right and left sides of the icon, one for the Coptic readings and the other for the Arabic. Black cloth is placed on each lectern and a lit candle is placed beside it on a candlestand.

No incense is offered during the first three days of the holy Pascha to symbolize Christ, our Paschal lamb, who was kept from the tenth to the fourteenth of Nissan.

From Paschal Wednesday until the eve of the Feast of Resurrection, the Church refrains from offering the liturgical kiss in commemoration of Judas' deceptive kiss by which he delivered his Master to the cross. Therefore, one does not kiss the hand of the priest or the bishop as they enter the church, during the raising of incense or at the close of the prayers and the readings.

The omission of the Reconciliation Prayer during the Liturgies of Maundy Thursday and Bright Saturday is another liturgical expression of sorrow to convey that the reconciliation of earth with heaven was only fulfilled in the resurrection of our Lord Jesus Christ's from the dead. Christ, to whom is due glory, has instituted this reconciliation as a Mediator between God and man in His incarnation, passion, crucifixion, resurrection, ascension to heaven, and sitting on the right hand of the Father, as a forerunner to us all.

These are some of the expressions of grief during the holy Paschal Week in addition to the multitude of delightful tunes during the week which bring us into an atmosphere of utter reverence. I do not say that they take us into an atmosphere of spiritual sadness, for experience has proven otherwise. The tunes communicate reverence to the soul, not sadness, as well as hopeful anticipation for glorious and unutterable joy. There is no tune that moves you to tears that does not immediately cause you to become joyful and cheerful. The rhythms are led by a marvellous inspiration that places the soul in a state of devotion tinged with holy sadness and melded with joy and hope, leading the soul to an unparalleled spiritual experience of harmony throughout the prayers. Taste and listen to how sweet the Church is!

The rites, prayers and artistic tunes of this week convey the congregation to a spiritual atmosphere the Church arranged. On the other hand, the excessive use of black cloths to cover the Church columns, walls, lecterns, and icons of the saints is an overdramatized expression of grief within the Church, unbeknownst to Eastern Christendom more generally and the Coptic Church, in particular, during the first millennium. The Eastern Church is a joyous Church, suffused by the joys of the resurrection occupying the heart of its entire liturgical year.

The older tradition of the Coptic Church excludes any outward expression of extreme mourning. Enveloping the Church, "the house of joy and cheer" and "the house of angles," with black cloths in the manner we see today is a western encroachment that has impinged on the East.

The Coptic Rites are described in all the churches of the world as simply, reverent, and majestic, which does not rely on external stimuli or splendour to stir the spirit of prayer within the believer.

Take, for example, the icons of the Coptic Church. One cannot find a single icon expressing suffering or pain. Even the icons of the martyrs portray them with joyful countenances because the Church dwells not transient pain, however brutal they may have been, as much as it focuses on the glories they gained through their passion. Furthermore, the Coptic Church portrays Christ crucified in a state of triumph instead of exaggerating the wounds of the nails and the spear with graphic depictions and an emaciated head and mangled face.

The Holy Bible always pairs suffering with joy and consolation, as this fulfils the Christ's Passion and Cross. The passions of the Cross are so intense that no sad, black colour could ever express them, for the greater the suffering the greater also the consolation we receive. "For just as the sufferings of Christ are abundant for us, so also our consolation is abundant through Christ." (2 Corinthians 1:5). Every suffering that does not produce joyful repentance is removed from the passion of Christ. "I often boast about you; I have great pride in you; I am filled with consolation; I am overjoyed in all our affliction." (2 Corinthians 7:4). It is also written "I am now rejoicing in my sufferings" (Colossians 1:24).

What we practice nowadays in our churches with all these black coverings is very different from the older Coptic tradition. How can we cover the icons of the saints with black cloth when they have inherited the land of joy and always behold Christ's face? How can we cover the lectern, over which we read the joyful Gospel of salvation, with black cloth from all sides? Even if the readings are focused on the Cross and the Passion, these are life-giving, saving passions.

The practice of using black coverings for the altar and black service vestments began appeared in the Middle Ages. There does not seem to be any documentation of it prior to that era. The following is what appeared in the oldest liturgical references about this rite. Ibn Sebā' says:

> They gather in the church to prepare what befits the Passion Week. This involves closing the door of the sanctuary, preparing the lectionaries containing the passages of Passion Week, putting a lectern in the middle of the second chorus and placing on it the opened Paschal Book covered with *green or blue cloth*, adorned with three

candles, which contains the readings from the Prophecies and the Gospels...[31]

Thus, it is evident here that at the time of Ibn Sebā' there was no mention of black cloth, but only green or blue.

The *Church Order Manuscript No. 118 (Rites) at the Patriarchate in Cairo*, which goes back to 1627 AM / 1911 AD mentions the following:

> They, then, return to the church at the time of the ninth hour of that day (i.e., Palm Sunday), close the doors to the altar, hang up a *black or coloured cloth* on the altar door, place the lectern in the middle, cover it with *black or coloured cloth*, open on it the Paschal Book covered with *black satin cloth or otherwise*, and begin praying the Holy Pascha.

It is obvious here that, according to the Church Order manuscript, the black colour is not a requirement during the Holy Paschal Week but could be replaced with any other colour. This can also be found in the other manuscripts under study.

It appears in Ibn Kabar's (d. 1324 AD) discourse about the "order of the Holy Pascha days" that "the doors to the altars are closed as is customary and the priests, the deacons and the entire laity move to the nave of the church where the prayers take place, for the Lord was brought outside of the city during His Passion. St. Paul

---

[31] Yoḥanna Ibn Zakaria Ibn Sebā', *op. cit.*, 326.

also says: "Let us then go to him outside the camp and bear the abuse he endured" (Hebrews 13:13). The pure disciples and saintly fathers have placed certain statutes and instructions for this Holy Week which they enjoined us to keep and warned against ignoring or wasting[32] any of them.

Furthermore, we find that Ibn Kabar (1324 AD) has mentioned the following lines during his exposition of the sanctification of the Holy Chrism, which at his time took place during the days of the Holy Pascha under Pope Theodosius, the 79th Patriarch of Alexandria, in the church of St. Mercurius in Old Cairo in 1299 AD. He explains how they placed a wooden altar on each side of the main altar, one for the chrism and the other for the olive oil, saying:

> ... then they placed on either side of the main altar two wooden altars which they have prepared for the Chrism. They covered the main altar and the two wooden alters with *black cloth*, and the patriarch donned a *black garment*... etc.[33]

He also mentions the following in his discussion on the sanctification of the Holy Chrism in 1305 AD in the

---

[32] This word was misspelled in the manuscript.
[33] Shams al-Riʾāsa Abū al-Barakāt Ibn Kabar, *The Lamp of Darkness and the Clarification of the Service* (*Miṣbāḥ al-ẓulma wa ʿīḍāḥ al-khidma*), Manuscript No. 203 (Arabic), National Library in Paris, Section 9, Folio 357.

Monastery of St. Macarius under Pope John VIII, the 80th Patriarch of the Coptic Church:

> It is customary when consecrating it in St. Macarius' Monastery to place two wooden altars in the Benjamin sanctuary, one to the south (right) of the main altar and the other to the north (left)[34], and all three altars are covered with *black cloths*. The patriarch and the bishops don *black garments*...[35]

Also:

> ... he (the pope) changes into a *black garment* for the Liturgy...[36]

Notice how the Chrism, which is the oil of joy and the mystery of the Holy Spirit – the Paraclete – is sanctified on an altar covered in black cloths. Even the patriarch and bishops are wearing black vestments! This should be disdained in the Church, which is heaven on earth. The altar coverings must always be white, and the service garments must remain white and washed, not

---

[34] It is quite obvious here that the right side of the altar is towards the south and the left side towards the north. In other words, the right side of the altar is also the right side of the priest serving before the altar and the left side of the altar is the left side of the priest.

[35] Shams al-Ri'āsa Abū al-Barakāt Ibn Kabar, *op. cit.*, Section 9, Folio 359.

[36] *Ibid.*, 362.

dyed with colours.[37] What we read here from Ibn Kabar is a new development that infiltrated the Church's practices during the Middle Ages. The first ten centuries did not observe any of these customs.

The patriarch wore black vestments and the holy altars were covered with black coverings during the consecration of the Holy Chrism because the latter came during the Holy Paschal Week. Hence, a confusion arose between the joy of consecrating the chrism and olive oils of joy and the Paschal Week of the Passions of the Cross, which is considered to be the week of sorrows and sufferings which the black colour befits. It is well established that the custom of consecrating the chrism during the Holy Paschal Week began in the year 970 AD under the Pope Mina II (956 – 974 AD), the 61st Patriarch of the Coptic Church. Before this time, it was

---

[37] Canon No. 28 of Pope Athanasius of Alexandria states: "The garments of the priests, wherein they celebrate, shall be *white and washed*. They shall be laid in the store-chambers of the sanctuary. At the hour of going to the altar they shall be found laid in the sanctuary, in the store-chamber, in charge of him that guards the vessels, even as the prophet Ezekiel has ordained."
Canon No. 96 of St. Basil the Great, which are Egyptian laws, states: "The garments wherein they celebrate shall not be brought outside of the church. They shall be kept in the store-chambers of the church servants or with the books. These are garments fit for priesthood and belong to the altar. These are *white garments, undyed with colour,* that go down to their feet." Refer also to Canon No. 106 of the same laws.

consecrated on the Last Friday of the Great Lent.[38] It is indeed a source of joy for our souls that the occasion of consecrating the Holy Chrism has returned to its original location after over a thousand years. It was consecrated seven times[39] during Pope Shenouda III's papacy starting in 1981 AD on the Thursday before the Last Friday of the Great Lent, which is the day on which the prayers of the General Unction are conducted. Pope John IXX (1928 – 1942) preceded him in doing so in the year 1930 AD during the Great Lent, not near its traditional date, but towards the middle of the lent.

In this manner the connection between the black altar drapes, the black service vestments and the Holy Paschal Week was broken. Even if we wear black or dark clothes during the service of the Holy Liturgy during the Holy Paschal Week, the angels surrounding the altar and filling the sanctuary will not remove their white garments.

Our excessive expression of grief by covering the Church with black drapes and cloths has led to other excessive decorations by adorning the Church with white and red decorations during Pentecost. Such

---

[38] With the one exception of 940 AD during the pontiff Pope Makkar I, 59th Patriarch of the Coptic Church.
[39] Pope Shenouda III has consecrated it six times in St. Bishoy Monastery in Al-Natron Valley in the years 1981, 1987, 1993, 1995, 2005 and 2008, and a seventh time in 2004 in Asmara, Eritrea.

external appearances cannot translate the spirit of joy in our souls, for the joy of the resurrection is an inward experiential joy which we receive in our hearts through the prayers, hymns, readings, and rites of the church. "He trampled down death by death, and upon those in the tombs He bestows life." This is the true joy that produces tears.

These excessive externalities, which have accrued through the years, have caused us to decorate the church for one other than Christ, its Master and Bridegroom. Unfortunately, we are inclined to decorate the church during the prayers of the Holy Crowning service with colourful decors that flash and sparkle in a distractive manner aside from the branches and flowers that are placed on the sides of the centre aisle of the church as if the house of God has been turned into a theatre or celebration hall. The house of the LORD, which is the house of repentance and sacraments, has been defiled by our ignorance, even if unintentional. We do not realise that the church is filled with angels and saints in the Lord's presence, being heaven itself for it is the dwelling place of God with His people. Thus, we ought to enter with reverence and trembling, rather than implementing whatever we might fancy.

The Holy Paschal Week in the Syriac Church of Antioch

The Syriac Church expresses its participation in the Lord's saving passions during this great week through liturgical rituals with their own spiritual connotations and understandings. The Church refrains from kissing the priest's or bishop's hand throughout the entire Holy Week, and not just from Wednesday as in the Coptic Church. It also refrains from kissing the Holy Gospels after the readings, during the raising of incense, the hourly prayers, and the Holy Liturgy. During this week, the Gospel is not chanted in the usual manner and the congregation abstains from the liturgical greeting. The prayer of peace, which corresponds to the reconciliation prayer in the Coptic Rite, is not prayed. They do not recite "Peace be with you all" in anticipation of the first word the LORD uttered after His holy resurrection "Peace be with you." The Syriac Church is also rich in poetically or non-poetically rhymed hymns that are chanted during this Holy Week.

The Syriac Church has prayers that are recited daily during the Paschal Week, among which is the following hymn:

> O Lord! Blessed is thy passion for our sakes and blessed is thy condescension for our sakes. O Lord, by thy great passion, have mercy on us and grant us thy blessing, that we may become sufferers of thy passion and heirs to thy salvation.

The Holy Paschal Week in the Byzantine Church

On the first three days of Pascha, that is Monday, Tuesday and Wednesday, the Byzantine Church celebrates a liturgical service called the προηγιασμένη "Progiasmeni," that is the "Presanctified Liturgies." This service is conducted for the reception of the Lord's Body and Blood when the Divine Liturgy should not be prayed,[40] as this is a period of contrition and ascetism, while the Divine Liturgy is considered a Paschal joy. However, they do not pray any memorials of the departed during this week. The Latin Church does not perform any funeral services during this week as well.[41]

In the Matins Prayer, the Greek Orthodox Church chants a common Tone 8 Troparion during the first three days of the Holy Pascha, saying:

> Behold the Bridegroom comes at midnight And blessed is the servant whom He shall find watching. And unworthy is he whom He shall find heedless. Beware, therefore, O my soul, lest you be worn down with sleep, lest you be given

---

[40] This liturgy does not include the full elements of the typical Divine Liturgy, especially the sanctification and anaphora. It was introduced by the Byzantine Patriarch Sergius in the year 615 AD. Back then, it was celebrated during the weekdays of the Great Lent, except on Saturdays, Sundays, the Feast of the Annunciation and Maundy Thursday. Nowadays, however, it is only celebrated on Wednesdays and Fridays of the Great Lent.

[41] Oswald H.E. KHS-Burmester, *The Egyptian or Coptic Church, A Detailed Description of her Liturgical Services and the Rites and Ceremonies Observed in the Administration of her Sacraments*, Publications de la Société d'Archéologie Copte. Textes et Documents (Cairo: Société d'archéologie copte, 1967), 270.

over unto death, and lest you be shut out of the kingdom. Wherefore arouse yourself and cry: Holy! Holy! Holy, are You O our God. Through the intercession of the Theotokos, Saviour save us.

PART TWO

Lazarus Saturday

Chapter One: The Miracle of Raising Lazarus from the Dead

Raising Lazarus from the Dead in Preparation of the Lord's Passion and Cross

Lazarus Saturday holds a distinct place in the liturgical calendar. The Eastern Churches have made the miracle of raising Lazarus[1] from the dead a foundation for entry into the events of the Holy Paschal Week.

---

[1] It was told in ancient stories that Lazarus was thirty years old when our Lord Jesus raised him from the dead, and that he lived for another thirty years afterwards. He departed in Cyprus in the year 63 AD and was laid near the city of Kition in a tomb bearing the inscription: "Lazarus, four days dead, beloved of Christ." In 890 AD, Emperor Leo VI of Byzantium had his honourable relics transferred to Constantinople. According to the Coptic Synaxarion, Lazarus was the first bishop of Cyprus. The Maronite Church in Cyprus celebrates the commemoration of Lazarus on the seventeenth day of March. It is mentioned that, after the Saviour's ascension to heaven, the Jews captured Lazarus and his two sisters and threw them into the sea. But God's grace transferred them to Marseille in France, where they preached the Gospel. According to an ancient tradition, Lazarus became bishop

The Eastern Churches have dedicated the day that separates Great Lent from the Paschal Week to celebrate the raising of Lazarus from the dead in preparation of Holy Week, although this miracle did not actually occur on the day before Christ entered Jerusalem. In fact, several events occurred between the Lord's raising of Lazarus from the dead until His triumphal entry into Jerusalem.

The reason the Church celebrates the miracle of raising Lazarus from the dead just before the beginning of the Paschal Week is that the Jewish chief priests and Pharisees plotted to kill Jesus because of this miracle, which exposed their dishonesty and dispersed their fame.

Furthermore, the Church wanted to teach us that the Lord, who accepts suffering unto death, is Himself the resurrection and the life. He is life itself and death has no authority over Him.

On Lazarus Saturday, the Lord revealed His divinity and ability to raise the dead, even from the abyss of the tomb and Hades. This enables us to enter the week of His paschal passion and life-giving death with the hope of passing over to life. The One who raises the dead

---

of Marseille and received the crown of martyrdom around the year 60 AD.

cannot be held captive by death but underwent death to abolish its sting. Therefore, before He accepted death in Himself, He rattled the might of death. When He raised Lazarus, He tormented death's sting, but when He died and rose, He destroyed its sting forever.

Hence, it was necessary that He raise Lazarus before embarking on the path to the cross. To strengthen the disciples' faith, lest it perish by the cross, the Lord brought hope of overcoming the adversity of affliction from the joy of raising Lazarus. Indeed, raising Lazarus from the dead has become a sign of what the Lord was about to accomplish in Himself.

When the Lord stood before the tomb, after the stone was rolled away, fearful silence shrouded everyone smelling death's scent. Then, Jesus cried with a loud voice "Lazarus, come out," and the dead man came out from the depths of Hades pursuing the voice of the great Son of God. The Lord could have called all the dead from their tombs in that same voice, saying "come out," and they would have all risen with Lazarus. But the Lord called Lazarus alone, postponing His call to the rest until He descended to them in Hades through the cross.

The miracle of raising Lazarus from the dead was the beginning of the end. It was due to this miracle that the events of the last hours of our Lord on earth ensued until the day of the Cross. What were these final events?

The Events that followed Raising Lazarus from the Dead

After the Lord raised Lazarus from the dead, some of the Jews who had witnessed the miracle went and told the chief priests and the Pharisees, who then plotted to put Jesus to death. Therefore, Jesus left Bethany and went to stay in Ephraim with His disciples. He no longer went and taught openly among the Jews.[2]

It seems that the period the Lord remained hidden was not a short one, although the Gospels did not mention how long it was. However, the chief priests and the Pharisees lost track of where He was.[3] But when the time came for Him to offer Himself as a sacrifice for the life of the whole world, having loved it to the end, He began His journey back to Jerusalem. Then children were brought to Him that He might lay His hands on them to bless them and pray.[4] When the disciples rebuked those who brought the children, Jesus stopped them and took the children in His arms, laid His hands on them, and blessed them, saying: "whoever does not

---

[2] John 11:53-54
[3] John 11:57
[4] Matthew 19:13

receive the kingdom of God like a child shall not enter it."[5]

On His way to the Cross, the Lord met with the wealthy young man whose riches caused him to stumble from carrying the cross. This young man's money prevented him from loving his neighbour. Likewise, the scribes and Pharisees who knew the entire law, preaching it to others, were not practicing it.[6] While they were boasting of keeping the law, they offended God by transgressing the law. Philo, the Jewish historian, mentions that when the angel of death came to take the spirit of Rabbi Chaninah, the latter said to the angel: go and retrieve the Talmud and see if I did not keep any of it.

On His way to Jerusalem, the Lord gave us the parable of the vinedressers and the vine,[7] in which the landowner rewarded equally those who worked only one hour in humility and those who bore the day's burden and the scorching heat with pride. The wages depended not on the quantity but the quality of the work, because no matter how righteous we are, we ought to say with heartfelt conviction: "We are unworthy servants; we have only done what was our

---

[5] Mark 10:13-16 and Luke 18:17
[6] Matthew 23:2-3
[7] Matthew 20

duty" (Luke 17:10). In any case, many are called, but few chosen.[8]

As they were going up to Jerusalem, Jesus was walking ahead and the disciples were following Him, marvelling and fearful.[9] So, for the third time, Jesus told them about His crucifixion, death, and resurrection,[10] but they did not understand it because it was hidden from them. They did not grasp what was said,[11] and they were afraid to ask Him about this saying.[12] How baffling! Until this moment, the disciples were bewildered, afraid, obtuse, and ignorant of the cross!

Then, the mother of the sons of Zebedee came up with her sons and, keeling before Him, asked Him to grant her sons, James and John, to sit one at His right hand and the other at His left hand in His kingdom. Had she known the burden of the road to His kingdom, she would have hidden herself with her sons, for who can endure the passions of the cross? When the other ten disciples grew indignant at them, Jesus proclaimed that He was about to give His life as a ransom for many[13].

---

[8] Matthew 22:14
[9] Mark 10:32
[10] Luke 18:31-34. The first time was in Luke 9:22, and the second time in Matthew 17:22-23 and in Mark 9:30-32 and in Luke 9:42-45. This third time came in Matthew 20:17-19, Psalm 10:32-34 and Luke 18:31-34.
[11] Luke 18:34
[12] Luke 9:45
[13] Matthew 20:28 and Mark 10:45

At this point, Jesus reached Jericho on Thursday, the seventh of Nissan, or Friday, the eighth of Nissan, being followed by a great crowd. There, he met with Zacchaeus the tax collector, became a guest in his house and saved his soul that was about to perish for the love of money.[14]

Then the Lord proceeded to tell the parable of the servants and the stewards since the crowd greatly felt that the Kingdom of God was at hand. However, the Lord revealed their inner guile when He mentioned in the parable that the nobleman "went into a far country." The Lord said this parable in light of the recurrent events in the history of the Jewish nation. Josephus mentioned that this happened twice in the time of Archelaus and in the time of Herod Antipas.

When Christ had said this, He went on ahead, going up to Jerusalem.[15] As He left Jericho, heading towards Jerusalem, He met with the blind Bartimaeus, sitting by the roadside, and He healed him. The blind man immediately received his sight and followed Jesus on

---

[14] Luke 19:1-10
[15] Luke 19:28. The road from Jericho to Jerusalem took about six hours, and it was a stony cliff used as a hiding place for thieves. On Jericho's side, the road was 600 feet above sea level, and on Jerusalem's side 3000 feet. It was about 25km long.

the way. The rebuke of the multitude did not silence him, but he seized his healing through his tenacity.[16]

On Saturday, the ninth of Nissan of the year 5534 of creation, Jesus came to Bethany – the house of sorrow, where Lazarus was, whom Jesus raised from the dead. There they prepared supper for Him in the house of Simeon the leper, and Mary rushed behind the Lord and anointed His feet with costly pure spikenard while He sat at the table, wiping His feet with her hair. The house was filled with the fragrance of the balm of love, the ointment of the Lord's burial. No one objected to this act except Judas who was stealing from the money box for the poor. The news soon broke out, and a great multitude came to see Jesus and Lazarus whom He had raised, and they believed in Jesus.[17]

At that time, Jews from all over the world filled Jerusalem, who came up to ritually purify themselves before the Passover.[18] Josephus mentions that there was about two million Jews at this time. The news of Christ's raising Lazarus from the dead after four days had spread among the crowd and was the centre of their conversation. The people wanted Jesus to come to the feast that they might see Him.[19]

---

[16] Mark 10:46-50
[17] John 12:11
[18] John 11:55
[19] Jon 11:56

This was a quick account of the events that followed raising Lazarus from the dead until the Lord had come to Bethany and His triumphant entry into Jerusalem.

Chapter Two: The Rites of the Lazarus Saturday Prayers

Introduction

We read the following in the *Church Order Manuscript No. 118 (Rites) in Cairo Patriarchate, 1911*:

> With the help of the Almighty God, we begin the second part of the Church Order which pertains to the Holy Paschal Week. We start with the order of Lazarus Saturday, which is read in the annual tune because of the commemoration of the Lord's great miracle of raising Lazarus from the dead. In the days of old, this was the Passover of the Forty Days.

The same is mentioned by the *Manuscript of Al-Baramūs Monastery for the year 1514*, which reads:

> On this day, we pray in the annual tune because of the commemoration of the Lord's great miracle of raising Lazarus from the dead. In the old days, this was the Passover of the Forty Days.[1]

First: The Midnight and Morning Praise of Lazarus Saturday

---

[1] Samuel of Shibīn Al-Qanater, *The Church Order as per the Patriarchate manuscripts in Cairo and Alexandria and the manuscripts of the monasteries and churches*, Part 3 (Cairo: 2000), 53.

The Batos Psali

In the Midnight Praise we chant the Batos Psali, a metrical hymn acrostically ordered after the Coptic alphabet, in which almost all the verses end with the name "Lazarus." This Psali tells the story of raising Lazarus in brief as it appeared in the Scriptures. It is thus different from the older Psalis which are usually a means of prayer, intercession, or veneration. However, this Psali adheres to that structure in its first couple of verses, which read:

- Come all to praise, and sing to the Lord Jesus Christ, the Logos, who raised Lazarus.
- Everyone glorifies You, O eternal Son, and glory befits You for You have raised Lazarus.

and another two verses later, which read:

- To You is glory and praise, O good Lover of mankind, with Your power raise us like Lazarus the just.
- Who is like You among the gods, O our good Saviour, with the power of Your divinity You raised Lazarus the just.

The author of the Psali describes himself in the final verse as "the poor servant." Its style evinces a post-fourteenth century authorship.

The *Manuscript of the Roman Quarter Typikon (15th century)* includes a Batos Psali for Lazarus Saturday in Coptic only, and it starts with ⲁⲓⲉⲣⲛⲟⲃⲓ `ⲱ ⲡⲓⲁⲅⲁⲑⲟⲥ:

I have sinned, O Good One, revive me O Son of God like Lazarus the just. Heal me O Jesus Christ…

It was written by Nicodemus, who mentions his name in the final stanza. After translating it into Arabic, I found that it does not introduce any new meanings, so I omitted it here.

The Batos and Adam Expositions

The Batos Exposition is read before the conclusion of the Theotokia. But Lazarus Saturday also has an Adam Exposition.[2] In these two expositions, Lazarus is surnamed "Lazarus the bishop," since, according to the Coptic Synaxarion, Lazarus was the first bishop of Cyprus.[3]

The Batos Exposition begins by saying:

> Let us go to Bethany and see these great signs and wonders that Jesus Christ performed among the crowd. Those who came to the Feast, the pilgrims and city inhabitants, they

---

[2] Adam Exposition – although Lazarus Saturday lies in the Batos days – Adam refers to the tune with which the exposition is read regardless of the Batos or Adam days of the week according to their current definitions. For example, all the expositions of the Holy Pascha days are in the Adam tune, while the exposition of the vespers of Resurrection Sunday is in the Batos tune. In either case, whether Batos or Adam, we are left with only the introduction and the first two verses of the expositions in Coptic. Even this small remnant is fading away, as it is customary to only read the expositions in Arabic nowadays. The reader will often read the Batos exposition followed immediately by the Adam one, thus repeating the core content of the exposition!

[3] *PO.*, t. XVI, fasc. 2, 418.

went and saw the resurrection that took place. For truly the King of peace was there, showing His power and the might of His authority. Come to us, O celibate, the son of thunder, the beloved of our Saviour, John the Son of Zebedee, to tell us about the joy of Mary and Martha and their only brother, Lazarus the righteous.

It then goes on to briefly portray the miracle of raising Lazarus from the dead, the great banquet of love that they prepared for the Saviour, and the flask of ointment that was poured on His head. Finally, the exposition concludes by saying:

> Pray to the Lord on our behalf, O beloved of Christ, Lazarus the bishop, that He may forgive us our sins.

On the other hand, the Adam Exposition repeats the same story once more but in more detail. It concludes by saying:

> Oh what a great wonder that surpasses the minds and fascinates perception. Our Master raised the widow's son in Nain at his burial and Jairus' daughter at the hour of her death. Those and many others have been raised from the dead on the day they died save Lazarus who was raised four days after his death and burial in the tomb. Through the prayers of Lazarus the bishop, O Lord, grant us the forgiveness of our sins. Amen.

Second: The Prayer of Matins Raising of Incense on Lazarus Saturday

The Batos Doxology

None of the Church Order manuscripts until 1911 include a Batos Doxology in the Matins Raising of Incense on Lazarus Saturday. This can also be found in the Annual Psalmody of Claudius Iohannes Labib (1868 – 1918) which was published in 1908 in Cairo, as well as in the Annual Psalmody of Fr Mina Al-Baramūsī (1925) which was published the same year in Alexandria.

On the other hand, the *Manuscript of the Roman Quarter Typikon (15th century)* includes a Batos Doxology in Coptic only, which was prayed in the Matins of Lazarus Saturday and starts with Ⲑⲱⲟⲩϯ ⲧⲏⲣⲟⲩ ⲱ̀ ⲛⲓⲡⲓⲥⲧⲟⲥ, which translates to: "Gather all you believers to praise our Lord Jesus Christ... etc."

The following is the original Coptic text and its translation into English:

Gather all you believers to praise our Lord Jesus Christ Who raised Lazarus with the power of His Divinity.	Ⲑⲱⲟⲩϯ ⲧⲏⲣⲟⲩ ⲱ̀ ⲛⲓⲡⲓⲥⲧⲟⲥ : ⲛ̀ⲧⲉⲛϩⲱⲥ ⲙ̀ⲡⲉⲛⲟ̅ⲥ̅ Ⲓⲏ̅ⲥ̅ Ⲡⲭ̅ⲥ̅ : ⲫⲏⲉⲧⲁϥⲧⲟⲩⲛⲟⲥ Ⲗⲁⲍⲁⲣⲟⲥ : ϧⲉⲛ ⲧϫⲟⲙ ⲛ̀ⲧⲉ ⲧⲉϥⲙⲉⲑⲛⲟⲩϯ .
Raise us with Your power from the shadow of death like the righteous Lazarus whom You raised after his death.	Ⲙⲁⲧⲟⲩⲛⲟⲥ(ⲧⲉⲛ) ϧⲉⲛ ⲧⲉⲕϫⲟⲙ : ⲉⲃⲟⲗϧⲉⲛ ⲧ̀ϧⲏⲓⲃⲓ ⲙ̀ ⲫⲙⲟⲩ : ⲙ̀ ⲫ̀ⲣⲏϯ ⲙ̀ⲡⲓ ⲉ̀ⲑⲙⲏⲓ Ⲗⲁⲍⲁⲣⲟⲥ : ⲫⲏⲉⲧ-ⲁⲕⲧⲟⲩⲛⲟⲥϥ ⲙⲉⲛⲉⲛⲥⲁ ⲡⲉϥⲙⲟⲩ .
You are the way and the life, O Jesus Christ the Creator. You	Ⲛ̀ⲑⲟⲕ ⲡⲉ ⲡⲓⲙⲱⲓⲧ ⲛⲉⲙ ⲡⲓⲱⲛϧ : ⲱ̀ Ⲓⲏ̅ⲥ̅ Ⲡⲭ̅ⲥ̅ ⲡⲓⲁⲏⲙⲓⲟⲣⲅⲟⲥ : ⲛ̀ⲑⲟⲕ

are the God the Life-Giver to Lazarus the righteous.	ⲡⲉ Ⲫϯ ⲉⲧϯ `ⲙ`ⲡⲱⲛϧ : `ⲛⲗⲁⲍⲁⲣⲟⲥ ⲡⲓⲇⲓⲕⲉⲟⲥ .
You are the resurrection, Who raised Lazarus the righteous. We ask You to deliver us from our afflictions and give us our share with him.	Ⲛⲑⲟⲕ ⲡⲉ ϯⲁⲛⲁⲥⲧⲁⲥⲓⲥ : ⲁⲕⲧⲟⲩⲛⲟⲥ `ⲙⲡⲓ`ⲑⲙⲏⲓ ⲗⲁⲍⲁⲣⲟⲥ : ⲧⲉⲛϯϩⲟ ⲛⲁϩⲙⲉⲛ ϧⲉⲛ ⲛⲉⲛⲑⲗⲩⲯⲓⲥ: ⲙⲟⲓ ⲛⲁⲛ ⲛⲉⲙⲁϥ `ⲛⲟⲩⲙⲉⲣⲟⲥ .
O believers, let us proceed to the Mount of Olives to Bethany to behold Lazarus the righteous, and to praise with hymns.	Ⲙⲁⲣⲉⲛϣⲉⲛⲁⲛ `ⲱ ⲛⲓⲡⲓⲥⲧⲟⲥ : `ⲉⲡⲓⲧⲱⲟⲩ `ⲛⲛⲓϫⲱⲓⲧ ϣⲁ Ⲃⲏⲑⲁⲛⲓⲁ : `ⲛⲧⲉⲛⲛⲁⲩ `ⲉⲡⲓ`ⲑⲙⲏⲓ ⲗⲁⲍⲁⲣⲟⲥ : ⲟⲩⲟϩ `ⲛⲧⲉⲛϩⲱⲥ ϧⲉⲛ ϩⲁⲛⲯⲁⲗⲓⲁ .
Let us praise and glorify, and worship the holy, and co-essential Trinity, who endures forever. We praise Him and glorify Him.	Ⲙⲁⲣⲉⲛϩⲱⲥ `ⲛⲧⲉⲛϯⲱⲟⲩ : ⲧⲉⲛⲟⲩⲱϣⲧ `ⲛϯ`ⲑⲣⲓⲁⲥ ⲉⲑⲟⲩⲁⲃ : ⲉⲥⲟⲓ `ⲛⲟⲙⲟⲟⲥⲓⲟⲥ ⲉⲑⲙⲏⲛ `ⲉⲃⲟⲗ ϣⲁ `ⲉⲛⲉϩ : ⲧⲉⲛϩⲱⲥ `ⲉⲣⲟϥ ⲧⲉⲛϯⲱⲟⲩ ⲛⲁϥ .
Pray to the Lord on our behalf, O my master the righteous father, Lazarus the bishop, that He may forgive us our sins.	Ⲧⲱⲃϩ ... : ⲡⲁϭⲥ `ⲛⲓⲱⲧ `ⲛⲇⲓⲕⲉⲟⲥ : ⲗⲁⲍⲁⲣⲟⲥ ⲡⲓ`ⲉⲡⲓⲥⲕⲟⲡⲟⲥ : `ⲛⲧⲉϥⲭⲁ ⲛⲉⲛⲛⲟⲃⲓ ⲛⲁⲛ `ⲉⲃⲟⲗ .

In the year 1920, Fr Philotheos Al-Makarī, Fr Barnabas Al-Baramūsī and Cantor Mikhail Jirjis published *The Typikon and Order of the Passion Week and the Glorious Passover Feast*. It was printed in the era of Pope Cyril V and included the same text of the aforementioned doxology in pages 10-12, which is to be prayed in the Matins Raising of Incense of Lazarus Saturday. However, it only shows the first six verses,[4] while the

---

[4] Cf. Yassa Abd Al-Masih, "Doxologies in the Coptic Church," cited by *BSAC*, t. IV, 1938, 106.

final verse, in which Lazarus is surnamed the bishop, came in the *Manuscript of the Roman Quarter Typikon (15th century)*.

It is quite peculiar that this good doxology is currently neglected and completely forgotten. Though a metrical doxology, it is not ordered after the Coptic alphabet, but mentions Lazarus in each of its verses and calls him "the righteous." It begins with praising Christ and concludes with praising the Trinity. In its entirety, it addresses the hypostasis of the Son, and therefore holds the same status as the doxologies of the lordly feasts, which precede the doxology of the ever-holy Virgin Lady and the other doxologies that follow.

On the other hand, the Batos Doxology prayed nowadays in the churches was first published in the Annual Psalmody which was printed by the Coptic Church Renaissance Association in Cairo in the year 1948. It is weaker in content than the former doxology in addition to not well cadenced. It calls Lazarus "St. Lazarus" – a title that thus far was not common in tradition. It also refers to him as "the bishop of Cyprus" as mentioned in the Coptic synaxarion. A quick recitation of the contents of both doxologies reveals that the first one conforms more to the spirit of prayer, as all its verses (except one) address the Lord Jesus Christ and the Holy Trinity, while the second one uses the third person singular form for addressing Lazarus himself.

The verses of this doxology read:
- Lazarus the bishop, the beloved of Christ, who was risen from the dead after four days.
- And he lived for forty years and became a bishop on the throne of Cyprus and tended the flock of Christ.
- Blessed are you O our holy father Lazarus the bishop for you were worthy to hear Jesus' voice, the God of the living and the dead.
- Rejoice O Lazarus the beloved for you were worthy of the episcopate; you tended the sheep, O great shepherd.
- We entreat you O our father to intercede on our behalf before Christ who has loved you and raised you from the dead.
- Pray to the Lord on our behalf, O shepherd of Christ, Lazarus the bishop, that He may forgive us our sins.

The Prophecies

The prophecies are read after Ⲫϯ ⲚⲀⲒ ⲚⲀⲚ (Evnoti nay nan), which was not mentioned in any of the Church Order manuscripts or the other manuscripts under study.

There are four prophecies of this day.

The First Prophecy is from the Book of Genesis (Gen 4:1-28) and contains Jacob's prophecy about his children's future in the end. This prophecy is read in the Greek Church on Palm Sunday Vespers during the Sunset Prayer on the evening of Lazarus Saturday.

This prophecy is closely tied to Lazarus Saturday, as Jacob speaks of his son Joseph:

> Joseph is a fruitful bough, A fruitful bough by a well; His branches run over the wall. The archers have bitterly grieved him, shot at him and hated him. But his bow remained in strength, and the arms of his hands were made strong by the hands of the Mighty God of Jacob.

It is a symbol of Christ, Whom the Jews plotted to kill but God raised Him from the dead, crushing the sting of death.

In this prophecy, we also read:

> The sceptre shall not depart from Judah… until Shiloh comes; and to Him shall be the obedience of the people. Binding his donkey to the vine, and his donkey's colt to the choice vine. He washed his garments in wine, and his clothes in the blood of grapes.

These connotations relate to Jesus' entry into Jerusalem, marking the beginning of the final stages of His passion for our salvation.

The Second Prophecy is from Isaiah (40:9-):

> O Zion, you who bring good tidings, get up into the high mountain. O Jerusalem, you who bring good tidings, gift up your voice with strength, lift it up, be not afraid. Say to

the cities of Judah, 'Behold your God!' Behold, the Lord God shall come with a strong hand, and His arm shall rule for Him. Behold, His reward is with Him, and His work before Him. He will feed His flock like a shepherd. He will gather the lambs with His arm...

The Third Prophecy is from Zephaniah (3:14 -):

Sing, O daughter of Zion! Shout, O Israel! Be glad and rejoice with all your heart, O daughter of Jerusalem! The Lord has taken away your judgments, He has cast out your enemy... In that day it shall be said to Jerusalem: "Do not fear; Zion, let not your hands be weak. The Lord your God in your midst, the Mighty One, will save. He will rejoice over you with gladness, He will quiet you with His love, He will rejoice over you with singing."

The Fourth Prophecy is from Zechariah (9:9-15):

Rejoice greatly, O daughter of Zion! Shout, O daughter of Jerusalem! Behold, your King is coming to you; He is just and having salvation, lowly and riding on a donkey, a colt, the foal of a donkey...

This fourth prophecy is also read in the Greek Church in the Sunset Prayer on the evening of Lazarus Saturday.

Hence, we can see that all the prophecies are preparing the hearts for Christ's entry into Jerusalem. Since the Church is not accustomed to reading prophecies on Sundays, and because of the paramount importance of the event we are about to celebrate, the prophecies pertaining to the Lord's entry into Jerusalem are read on the Saturday preceding the feast. Although prophecies are not typically read on Saturday, this exception is repeated only on the following Saturday – Bright Saturday – when the prophecies for the Resurrection are read after the Liturgy.

The Psalm of the Matins Gospel of Lazarus Saturday
The Psalm reads:

> O Lord, You have brought up my soul from Sheol, restored me to life from among those gone down to the Pit. You have turned for me my mourning into dancing. You have loosed my sackcloth and girded me with gladness (Psalm 29:3,11).

This is a wonderful psalm in terms of how it applies to the miracle of raising Lazarus from the dead. It is as if Lazarus himself chants this psalm immediately after the Lord set him free from the bondage of death and brought him up from Hades. In fact, it better complements the Liturgy Gospel than the Matins Gospel.

The Matins Gospel of Lazarus Saturday
The reading is from the Gospel of St. Luke the Evangelist (Luke 18:35-43) about the Lord healing Bartimaeus the blind man. This is the last miracle that Jesus performed

as He came out of Jericho and passed by Bethany on His way to Jerusalem.

The Matins Gospel Response of Lazarus Saturday

The *Manuscript of the Syrian Monastery for the year 1698* includes the following Matins Gospel Response of Lazarus Saturday, which corresponds to the text of the Holy Gospel:[5]

| A blind man in Jericho, named Bartimaeus, cried out before Him and proclaimed and said: | Ⲣⲱⲙⲓ ʼⲙⲃⲉⲗⲗⲉ ⲉⲧ ϧⲉⲛ Ⲓⲉⲣⲓⲭⲱ : ʼ ⲉⲡⲉϥⲣⲁⲛ ⲡⲉ Ⲡⲉⲣⲧⲓⲙⲉⲟⲥ : ⲁϥⲱϣ ʼ ⲉⲃⲟⲗ ʼⲙⲡⲉϥʼⲙⲑⲟ : ʼⲙⲡⲁⲓⲣⲏϯ ⲁϥϫⲱ ʼⲙⲙⲟⲥ . |
| Hearken to me for I have no eyes, and in Your name I believed. He put His hand on his eyes, and he received his sight and followed Him. | Ⲥⲱⲧⲉⲙ ʼⲉⲣⲟⲓ ϫⲉ ϯⲁⲧⲃⲁⲗ : ⲡⲉⲕⲣⲁⲛ ⲁⲓⲛⲁϩϯ ʼⲉⲣⲟϥ : ⲁϥⲭⲁ ⲧⲉϥϫⲓϫ ʼ ⲛⲛⲉϥⲃⲁⲗ : ⲁϥⲛⲁⲩ ʼⲉⲃⲟⲗ ⲁϥⲙⲟϣⲓ ʼ ⲛⲥⲱϥ. |

The Concluding Canon of the Matins Raising of Incense of Lazarus Saturday

The *Church Order Manuscript No. 118 (Rites) in the Cairo Patriarchate for the year 1911,* along with the other manuscripts under study, mention that in the Concluding prayers of Matins, the following canon is

---

[5] Samuel of Shibīn Al-Qanater, *op. cit.,* 55.

recited either in the Tune of Paul, the tune of ⲪⲎ `ⲈⲦⲀⲨ` ⲬⲪⲞϤ or the tune of ϨⲒⲦⲈⲚ ⲠⲒ `ⲰⲖⲎⲖ.[6]

The believers from every race praise the Lord of hosts, who raised Lazarus to life after his death.	ⲄⲈⲚⲞⲤ ⲚⲒⲂⲈⲚ `ⲚⲚⲒⲠⲒⲤⲦⲞⲤ : ϨⲰⲤ `Ⲉ ⲠⲞⲤ `ⲚⲦⲈ ⲚⲒⲬⲞⲘ : ⲪⲎⲦⲀϤⲦⲞⲨⲚⲞⲤ ⲖⲀⲌⲀⲢⲞⲤ : ⲘⲈⲚⲈⲚⲤⲀ ⲠⲈϤⲘⲞⲨ `Ⲉ`ⲠⲰⲚϨ .
Let us come to worship Him, and confess to Him, proclaiming and saying, "You are the Christ, the Son of God, the Giver of life to those who believe in Your holy name."	ⲀⲘⲰⲒⲚⲒ ⲦⲈⲚⲞⲨⲰϢⲦ `ⲘⲘⲞϤ : ⲦⲈⲚⲈⲢ `ⲞⲘⲞⲖⲞⲄⲒⲚ `ⲘⲘⲞϤ : ⲈⲚⲰϢ `ⲈⲂⲞⲖ `ⲘⲠⲀⲒⲢⲎϮ ⲈⲚⲬⲰ `ⲘⲘⲞⲤ : `ⲚⲐⲞⲔ ⲠⲈ ⲠⲬⲤ ⲨⲤ ⲐⲤ : ⲪⲎⲦϮ `ⲘⲠⲒⲰⲚϨ ` ⲚⲚⲎⲈⲐⲚⲀϨϮ `ⲈⲠⲈⲔⲢⲀⲚ ⲈⲐⲨ .
Glory be to the Father and the Son and the Holy Spirit.	ⲆⲞⲜⲀ ⲠⲀⲦⲢⲒ ...
For the sake of Your compassions, O Jesus Christ our Saviour, raise us with Your power from the death of sin, like You raised Lazarus from the tomb after four days.	ⲈⲐⲂⲈ ⲚⲈⲔⲘⲈⲦϢⲈⲚϨⲎⲦ : ⲒⲎⲤ ⲠⲬⲤ ⲠⲈⲚⲤⲰⲢ ⲘⲀⲦⲞⲨⲚⲞⲤⲦⲈⲚ ϦⲈⲚ ⲦⲈⲔⲬⲞⲘ : `ⲈⲂⲞⲖϦⲈⲚ `ⲪⲘⲞⲨ `ⲚⲦⲈ ` ⲪⲚⲞⲂⲒ : `Ⲙ`ⲪⲢⲎϮ `ⲈⲦⲀⲔⲦⲞⲨⲚⲞⲤ ⲖⲀⲌⲀⲢⲞⲤ : `ⲈⲂⲞⲖϦⲈⲚ ⲠⲒ`ⲘϨⲀⲨ : ⲘⲈⲚⲈⲚⲤⲀ ⲠⲒⲆ `Ⲛ`ⲈϨⲞⲞⲨ .
Now and forever and unto the age of all ages. Amen.	ⲔⲈ ⲚⲨⲚ ...
Take away from us the destructive slumber of sleep, and do not forsake us O Lord for we are the work of Your hands. We believe in Your life-giving divinity, who gave life to the mortal Lazarus.	ⲰⲖⲒ `ⲈⲂⲞⲖ ϨⲀⲢⲞⲚ `ⲘⲠⲒϨⲨⲚⲒⲘ ` ⲚⲦⲈ ϮⲈⲂϢ`Ⲓ `ⲚⲢⲈϤⲦⲀⲔⲞ : ` ⲘⲠⲈⲢⲬⲀⲚ `ⲚⲤⲰⲔ ⲠⲞⲤ : ⲬⲈ ⲀⲚⲞⲚ ⲚⲒ`ϨⲂⲎⲞⲨ`Ⲓ `ⲚⲦⲈ ⲚⲈⲔⲬⲒⲬ : ⲀⲚⲞⲚ ⲚⲒⲠⲒⲤⲦⲞⲤ ϦⲈⲚ ⲦⲈⲔⲘⲈⲐⲚⲞⲨϮ : ⲠⲒⲢⲈϤⲦⲀⲚϦⲞ ⲪⲎ`ⲈⲦⲀϤⲰⲚϦ : ` ⲚⲖⲀⲌⲀⲢⲞⲤ ⲪⲎⲈⲦⲀⲘⲞⲨ.

---

[6] This is also confirmed in the *Manuscript of Al-Baramūs Monastery for the year 1514.*

Now...

We say: O our Lord Jesus Christ, You are the resurrection and the life as You have said to Martha, Lazarus's sister, and You have fulfilled the word with Your action, proclaiming with a loud voice saying: "Lazarus come forth."

Now...

For You are truly the Creator of nature. Be kind to us with Your mercy and grant us a share with Lazarus Your beloved, the blessed and righteous one, in the region of the living.

Now...

O Jesus Christ, the Saviour, You speak with Your mercy to those who believe in You, that they may be granted eternal life. We, Your people, confess Your lordship. Have mercy upon us according to Your great mercy.

We proclaim saying...

Ke nyn ...

Ⲣⲱⲟⲛ ⲡⲉⲛⲟ̄ⲥ̄ Ⲓⲏ̄ⲥ̄ Ⲡⲭ̄ⲥ̄ : ʼⲛⲑⲟⲕ ⲡⲉ ϯⲁⲛⲁⲥⲧⲁⲥⲓⲥ : ⲛⲉⲙ ⲡⲓⲱⲛϧ ⲕⲁⲧⲁ ⲡⲉⲕⲥⲁϫⲓ : ʼⲉⲘⲁⲣⲑⲁ ʼⲧⲥⲱⲛⲓ ʼⲛⲖⲁⲍⲁⲣⲟⲥ : ⲟⲩⲟϩ ⲁⲕϫⲱⲕ ʼⲉⲃⲟⲗ ʼⲙⲡⲓⲥⲁϫⲓ ⲛⲉⲙ ʼⲡϩⲱⲃ : ⲉⲕⲱϣ ʼⲉⲃⲟⲗ ϧⲉⲛ ⲟⲩⲛⲓϣϯ ʼⲛʼⲥⲙⲏ : ϫⲉ Ⲗⲁⲍⲁⲣⲟⲥ ʼⲁⲙⲟⲩ ʼⲉⲃⲟⲗ.

Ke nyn ...

Ⲅⲉ ⲅⲁⲣ ʼⲛⲑⲟⲕ ⲁⲗⲏⲑⲱⲥ : ⲡⲓⲣⲉϥⲑⲁⲙⲓⲟ ʼⲛⲧⲉ ⲛⲓⲫⲩⲥⲓⲥ : ϣⲁⲛⲁʼϩⲑⲏⲕ ⲇⲉ ʼⲉʼϩⲣⲏⲓ ʼⲉϫⲱⲛ : ϧⲉⲛ ⲡⲉⲕⲛⲁⲓ ⲁⲣⲓⲟⲩʼⲓ ʼⲛⲛⲉⲛⲙⲉⲣⲟⲥ ⲛⲉⲙ Ⲗⲁⲍⲁⲣⲟⲥ ⲡⲉⲕⲙⲉⲛⲣⲓⲧ : ⲡⲓⲇⲓⲕⲉⲟⲥ ⲉⲧʼⲥⲙⲁⲣⲱⲟⲩⲧ : ϧⲉⲛ ʼⲧⲭⲱⲣⲁ ʼⲛⲧⲉ ⲛⲏⲉⲧⲟⲛϧ.

Ke nyn ...

Ⲓⲏ̄ⲥ̄ Ⲡⲭ̄ⲥ̄ ⲡⲓⲣⲉϥⲛⲟϩⲉⲙ : ʼⲛⲑⲟⲕ ⲁⲕϫⲱ ϧⲉⲛ ⲡⲉⲕⲛⲁⲓ : ϫⲉ ⲫⲏⲉⲑⲛⲁϩϯ ʼⲉⲣⲟⲕ : ʼⲛⲧⲉϥϭⲓ ʼⲛⲟⲩⲱⲛϧ ʼⲛʼⲉⲛⲉϩ : ⲏⲡⲡⲉ ⲁⲛⲟⲛ ⲡⲉⲕⲗⲁⲟⲥ : ⲉⲧⲉⲣʼⲟⲙⲟⲗⲟⲅⲓⲛ ϧⲉⲛ ⲧⲉⲕⲙⲉⲧⲟ̄ⲥ̄ : ⲛⲁⲓ ⲛⲁⲛ ⲕⲁⲧⲁ ⲡⲉⲕⲛⲓϣϯ ʼⲛⲛⲁⲓ.

Ⲉⲛⲱϣ ʼⲉⲃⲟⲗ ...

Third: The Liturgy Service of Lazarus Saturday

The following passage is mentioned in the *Church Order Manuscript No. 118 (Rites) in Cairo Patriarchate for the year 1911*:

> The Liturgy Service is practiced as usual, then, after Alleluia ⲫⲁⲓ ⲡⲉ ⲡⲓˋⲉϩⲟⲟⲩ (Vai Pe) and the Gospel Reading, they respond saying: Hail to Lazarus whom He raised after four days. Raise my heart, O my Lord Jesus, that was killed by the evil one.[7]

The Liturgy Readings of Lazarus Saturday

The Pauline reading (1 Corinthians 2:1-8) focuses on the fact that Christ's actions on this day were in demonstration of the Spirit and of power so that the faith of the crowd might not rest in the wisdom of men but in the power of God. The reading from the Catholic Epistle (1 Peter 1:25 – 2:6) came as a natural continuation of the Pauline, as it reads: "That word is the good news which was preached to you..." This is the God we preached to you, the One who has the power to raise from the dead. The Praxis reading (Acts 27:38 – 28:10) tells of St. Paul's final journey to Rome and the dangers he confronted as he escaped death twice, once in the sea and another time from the viper that fastened to his hand.

---

[7] The manuscript only includes the Coptic text of this passage.

The Psalm of the Liturgy Gospel of Lazarus Saturday
The Psalm of the Liturgy Gospel reads:

> The blessing of the LORD be upon you. We bless you in the name of the LORD. Many a time they have afflicted me from my youth. Yet they have not prevailed against me. (Psalm 129:2,8)

The first part of the psalm was the customary greeting that Jews exchanged when they passed by each other. This is what happened with Bartimaeus when he inquired of those who passed by about the incoming crowd. The second part shows what the blind man would be thinking when those who preceded Jesus' procession tried to silence him but could not. His faith and persistence caused him to receive healing and salvation, and he immediately followed Jesus. Hence, we can see that this psalm relates more to the Matins Gospel than the Liturgy Gospel.

The Liturgy Gospel of Lazarus Saturday
As is the case in all the rites of Eastern Churches for this day,[8] the Gospel Reading focuses on the miracle of raising Lazarus from the dead (John 11:1-45).

The Liturgy Gospel Response of Lazarus Saturday

---

[8] Oswald H.E. KHS-Burmester, *op. cit.*, 271.

It reads:

> Hail to Lazarus whom He raised after four days. Raise my heart, O my Lord Jesus, that was killed by the evil one.

This response came in the *Church Order Manuscript No. 118 (Rites) in Cairo Patriarchate for the year 1911*, the *Manuscript of Al-Baramūs Monastery for the year 1514*, and the *Manuscript of the Syrian Monastery for the year 1698*. It is also mentioned in the other manuscripts under study but using the first-person narrative, that is to say, "whom You raised ⲫⲏⲉⲧⲁⲕⲧⲟⲩⲛⲟⲥ" instead of "whom He raised ⲫⲏⲉⲧⲁϥⲧⲟⲩⲛⲟⲥϥ."[9]

The Adam Aspasmos of Lazarus Saturday

The *Manuscript of the Roman Quarter Typikon (15th century)* includes an Aspasmos to be read in the Liturgy Service of Lazarus Saturday, and labels it "Aspasmos from the Monday Psali." It only mentions its beginning, Ⲛⲓⲙ ⲅⲁⲣ ϧⲉⲛ ⲛⲓⲛⲟⲩϯ, that is "Who among the gods is likened unto You, O Lord. You are the true God, the Performer of miracles," which is the thirteenth verse of the Monday Psali.

This same Aspasmos is mentioned in *The Typikon and Order of the Passion Week and the Glorious Passover Feast,*

---

[9] Samuel of Shibīn Al-Qanater, *op. cit.*, 56.

published in 1920, but the latter adds to it the fourteenth verse of the aforementioned Psali, which reads:

> Blessed are You indeed, O my Lord Jesus, with Your good Father, and the Holy Spirit.

The Distribution Hymns of Lazarus Saturday
The *Church Order Manuscript No. 118 (Rites) in Cairo Patriarchate for the year 1911* mentions the following:

> At the time of distributing the Holy Sacrament, this Parallax is prayed in the annual tune.[10] The person chosen should read it for Lazarus.

Furthermore, the *Manuscript of the Roman Quarter Typikon (15th century)* speaks about it saying:

> It is read during the distribution in the annual tune. If the person chosen is not competent at reading it in the annual tune, it can be read in the manner of the Parallax. But it is better to be read in the annual tune after the old tradition.

The Typikon and Order of the Passion Week and the Glorious Passover Feast (1920) gives this Parallax the title "Distribution Hymn in the Annual Tune."

The *Manuscript of Abba Shenoute Typikon (14th century)* clarifies that this Parallax is to be read during the

---

[10] The manuscript gives this Parallax the title "Watos Doxology."

distribution after chanting Psalm 150, and then is followed by ` ˋK ̀cмаpшоүт.

The *Manuscript of the Hanging Church Typikon (16th century)* calls it the "canon" by saying "this canon is used during the time of distributing the Holy Sacrament."

This Parallax is made up of fourteen verses with the refrain "Lazarus come forth" being read after each verse.

Here is the text of these verses:
- "Lazarus come forth!" Christ called to You with His life-giving voice, saying "Lazarus come forth!"
- Lazarus died and was buried in the tomb for four days. The Lord's voice reached him, saying "Lazarus come forth!"
- The crowd which gathered there to comfort his sister heard the Lord, saying "Lazarus come forth!"
- Martha said to our Lord Jesus: "Had You been here my brother would have not died, but I know You will call him, saying 'Lazarus come forth'."
- Our Lord said to her: "If you believe in Me, then behold I will call him, saying 'Lazarus come forth'."
- "I believe that You are the Son of God, who is able to call him out by Your might, saying 'Lazarus come forth!'"
- Saying this He lifted His eyes to His good Father, crying out with a great voice, saying "Lazarus come forth!"
- The evil legions, who bound him in servitude in the depth of depths, said "Who is this who spoke, saying 'Lazarus come forth.'"
- Who is this whose voice broke the shackles of the bound and told him without fear, saying 'Lazarus come forth!'

- Rise leave him and flee; this is the Life-Giver to the dead. He revealed His voice and ordered him, saying 'Lazarus come forth!'"
- Immediately Lazarus came out, bound in linen, when the Lord called him, saying "Lazarus come forth!"
- Those who came to Mary believed because of what He had done, and because of the voice they heard, saying "Lazarus come forth!"
- Let us gather and praise our Lord Jesus Christ, and cry out to Him who said, "Lazarus come forth!"
- Forgive us our iniquities and grant us salvation through the prayers and intercessions of our Lady St. Mary.

In this manner, the Church provides a liturgical atmosphere of reverence to its children through the contents of the prayers of this day – I intended to mention most of them here. This atmosphere enables us to live the day's events and feel our place in it, especially when we partake of the Eucharistic Sacrifice, in which we receive Christ inside us as He becomes the resurrection of us all.

PART THREE

The Feast of Palm Sunday

Chapter One: About the Feast of Palm Sunday and its Liturgical Observances

Introduction
Ibn Kabar (1324 AD) mentions:

> Palm Sunday is the seventh Sunday of Lent, the conclusion of the holy forty days. In the days of old, when the fasting of the holy forty days started on the twelfth of Tobi and ended on the twenty-first of Meshir, Palm Sunday was the Passover of the fast, as opposed to the Resurrection Passover. The Holy Week would then be celebrated separately during the month of Nissan and the Resurrection Passover Feast celebrated on Sunday at the end of the Week, with the caveat that it did not coincide with the Jewish Passover Feast. This practice continued until the days of Pope Demetrius, the 12th Patriarch of

Alexandria[1]... The order of this feast[2] is mentioned in the chapter about fasting[3] as its conclusion.[4]

The Eastern Churches use the term "Hosanna Feast" to refer to this feast, where the word "Hosanna" is derived from the Aramaic word "hoshʿana," meaning "save us." In Greek, the word ὡσαννά (hosanna), has the same meaning.

On the other hand, the Latins call it "the feast of branches." In Eastern Churches, it is considered a carnival for children, who fill churches while carrying palms in their hands that they, themselves or with the help of others, weave into beautiful shapes. In fact, not having these children in church this day would result in the loss of an important aspect of this great feast, for it was children that filled the city with cheer before Christ as He meekly entered Jerusalem riding on a donkey.

---

[1] The separation of the fasting of the Holy Week from the Great Lent remained till the time of Pope Athanasius the Apostolic (328 – 373 AD), and not that of Pope Demetrius the Vinedresser (189 – 231 AD) as mentioned by Ibn Kabar. I have provided proof for this fact in my book "The Fast of Nineveh and the Great Holy Lent" if you wish to refer to it.

[2] i.e., the feast of Palm Sunday

[3] This is Chapter 18 of the book, *The Lamp that Lights in the Darkness In Clarifying the Service (Miṣbāḥ al-ẓulma wa ʿīdāḥ al-khidma)*.

[4] Manuscript No. 203 (Arabic) at the National Library of Paris, which corresponds to Section 19 of Ibn Kabar's book, *The Lamp that Lights in the Darkness In Clarifying the Service (Miṣbāḥ al-ẓulma wa ʿīdāḥ al-khidma)*.

When the chief priests tried to hamper the feast's spontaneity and genuineness by issuing an order to silence the children, the Lord answered them saying: "Have you never read, 'Out of the mouth of babes and nursing infants You have perfected praise'?" (Matthew 21:61). Whenever something is initiated by children, spontaneity prevails, and every mummery of piety vanishes. Therefore, Christ wanted His entry into Jerusalem to be unprompted, and not subject to the regulations of co-ordinators, so that it may bring joy to those of simple hearts, for the Lord said: "whoever does not receive the kingdom of God like a child shall not enter it" (Mark 10:15) (Luke 18:17).

With Christ on His Way to Jerusalem
On Sunday, the tenth of Nissan, Jesus left Bethany going to Jerusalem, riding on a colt, the foal of an ass, on which no one ever sat, for He is a new and meek King of a New Covenant.

The expression "an ass and a colt, the foal of an ass" reveals that it was necessary for the colt to have his mother accompany it to complete this service, as it was not yet trained to carry someone, since no one had ever sat on it.

When the large crowd coming to the feast heard Jesus was coming to Jerusalem, they took palms, which is only mentioned in the Gospel of St. John, and cut branches from the trees (olive branches) and spread them on the road. They also took off their garments and spread them on the road. The procession got spontaneously marshalled with a great multitude of all ages, including children, going on before Jesus, spreading their garments and olive branches on the road, and holding palms in their hands, while cheering and rejoicing. Another great crowd was following Jesus' procession and responded to the cheers of those who went on before Him.[5] Jesus rode in the midst of the crowd, surrounded by cheers and praises in the first ever antiphon in which the voice of children dominated those of the rest of the crowd.

As the procession drew near to Jerusalem and its great temple, at the descent of the Mount of Olives, the whole multitude of the disciples began to rejoice and praise God with a loud voice, saying: "Blessed is the King who comes in the name of the Lord! Peace in heaven and glory in the highest!" (Luke 19:38) "Hosanna to the Son of David! Hosana in the highest!" (Matthew 21:9) "Blessed is the kingdom of our father David that is coming in the name of the Lord!" (Mark 11:10). The crowd was also bearing witness to Jesus that he had called Lazarus out of the tomb and raised him from the dead (John 12:7).

---

[5] Refer to Mark 11:9 and Matthew 21:9.

While the crowd was amid celebration, Jesus looked at the city that appeared before Him with its vanity and lavish temple and wept over it.[6] It is a striking contrast. The crowd is rejoicing, and Jesus is weeping. He is weeping over the city that was receiving Him shouting "Hosanna, Hosanna," that is "save us now, save us now," but did not know what it was saying. Indeed, He was about to save it, not with cheering, but with the trial of the cross and the glory of the resurrection.

And when He entered Jerusalem, the entire city was stirred[7]. Why wouldn't it when the day of its destruction was at hand? As Jesus and His procession drew near to the temple, the disciples' cheers and praises mingled with those of the children.[8] The Pharisees then said to one another: "You see that you can do nothing; look, the world has gone after Him" (John 12:19). Jesus entered the temple near evening time.[9] They brought to Him the blind and lame in the temple, and He healed them[10] amidst the incessant cries of the disciples and praises of the children. So, the chief priests, the scribes and the Pharisees said to him: Rebuke Your disciples. Do you hear what these children are saying?[11] And Jesus said to

---

[6] Refer to Luke 19:41
[7] Refer to Matthew 21:10
[8] Refer to Matthew 21:15
[9] Refer to Mark 11:11
[10] Refer to Matthew 21:14
[11] Refer to Luke 19:39 and Matthew 21:16

them: If the disciples become silent, the very stones would cry out.[12] As for the children "have you never read, 'Out of the mouth of babes and sucklings You have perfected praise'?" (Matthew 21:16).

"And when He (Jesus) had looked round at everything, as it was already late, He went out to Bethany with the twelve" (Mark 11:11).

The Paradox of the Holy Paschal Week
The paradox of the entire Paschal Week is that the Church rejoices in her suffering Christ! Why wouldn't she when He has lifted her sorrow? In His weakness and suffering, the Church praises Him saying, "Yours is the power and the glory." When He is raised on the cross and after He bows His head and gives up the Spirit, she calls Him saying, "O only-begotten Son, the eternal and immortal Word of God. Holy Mighty, who by weakness showed forth what is great than power." When He was being taken down from the cross to be placed in the tomb, she chants His burial hymn saying, "Your throne, O God, is forever and ever. A sceptre of righteousness is the sceptre of Your kingdom."[13] This hymn expresses the perplexity of the Church: should she grieve over the death of her Bridegroom or rejoice over her salvation?

---

[12] Refer to Luke 19:40
[13] This hymn is called Πεκ`ϴροΝοс (Pek Ethronos)

Therefore, the tunes of this hymn are a blend of both expressions.

Moreover, the Saturday which the Lord spent in the depths and darkness of the tomb, the Church calls "Bright and Joyful Saturday." This is the mystery of Christ's death, the death that granted us life. Have you ever heard of funeral tunes that bring joy and quietness to the soul? Come and listen to them in the Coptic Church during the Holy Paschal Week. Is this not what St. Paul was referring to when he said: "I rejoice in my sufferings"?

The Meaning of the Word "Hosanna": ὡσαννά; – Save us now

"Hosanna" is the Greek verbalisation of the Hebrew word "hosh'ana," which is made up of two syllables: the first "hoshe" means "save – rescue – deliver," while the second "na" indicates the intensity of the need.

Thus, the literal meaning of the word is "save now." The early roots of this word in the Old Testament can be found in the Book of Psalms "Save us (Hosanna), we beseech You, O Lord! O Lord, we beseech You, deliver us (Hosanna)!" (Psalm 118:25). The origin of the word has a Messianic meaning, a form of entreating for salvation "save us."[14] This meaning is supported by the Talmud.

In the annual celebration of the Feast of Renewal, this word "Hosanna" became a special cheer specific to this feast, in which the people memorialized the salvation God performed for them. The longing of the people was for God to send them a saviour, like Judah Maccabee, who would grant them political freedom and renew the spiritual life.

In addition to this Messianic connotation of the word, it is also used as an expression of joy and praise. As the latter meaning spread, the word almost lost its original significance, becoming merely a cry of joy. It was used with this latter understanding in the most joyful Jewish feast, the "Feast of Tabernacles," to the extent that the seventh day of the feast was called the "Great Hosanna" or the "Hosanna Day."[15] However, using it as an expression of joy, thanksgiving and praise does not negate its original meaning as a plea for salvation.

Hence, the spiritually inspired people used this word in its originally profound meaning on the day the Lord entered Jerusalem as the Messiah coming in fulfilment of Zechariah's prophecy (9:9). Likewise, it was the

---

[14] Psalm 86:2 and Jeremiah 31:7
[15] *Theological Dictionary of the New Testament*, Volume IX, 682.

children's cry to Christ when He cleansed the temple,[16] but the crowd did not fully understand its original meaning. Rather they chanted it as a praise of thanksgiving and requesting deliverance from the yoke of the Romans. The word "Hosanna" appeared six times in the Holy Bible.[17]

If we return to the crowd's cheer according to the Gospel of St. Matthew, we find that it was "Hosanna to the Son of David." So, let us explore what the expression "to the Son of David" means. It is very likely that the crowd's cheer was in Hebrew – their national and sacred language – which indicates that the people used the Hebrew letter "lamed," which corresponds to the English letter "L," before the term "Son of David." The linguists have shown that this letter can be used as the calling letter "O," forming the following translation for the cheer: "Save us, O Son of David." However, the Greek script of this expression does not carry the meaning "O Son of David." Since the word "Hosanna" became more of an expression of the joy of salvation, which Christ had already instituted by His death and resurrection, than a plea for help, rendering the sense of the expression that came in the Gospel of St. Matthew as: "Glory be to the One Who has granted us salvation. Glory to the Son of David." The word "Hosanna" in the

---

[16] Refer to Matthew 21:9-15, Mark 11:9-10 and John 12:13.
[17] *The Biblical Knowledge Society*, Volume 1, 554.

Gospel of St. Matthew carries all the Messianic expectations and hopes that were fulfilled in Jesus.

"Hosanna" in Church Liturgy and Tradition

The word "Hosanna" entered the Church prayers very early on, and carried the connotation of praise, not in the sense of entreaty which the Churches used. The *Didache*, which records the liturgical prayers as practiced by the early church when it began celebrating the Lord's Supper, includes the following passage:

> Let grace come and let this world pass away. Hosanna to the Son of David. If anyone is holy let him come; if anyone is not, let him repent. Maranatha. Amen.
> (Didache 10:6)

It is obvious that the previous passage is not drawn up from the Gospels but was passed on through the liturgical tradition practiced by the Lord's disciples as they taught it to the early church.

Eusebius of Caesarea points out in his book, *Ecclesiastical History*, that for the early Christians, the word "Hosanna" was linked to the expectation of the imminent coming of the Lord. When the Jews set James the Apostle, the bishop of Jerusalem, on the pinnacle of the temple just before his martyrdom, "he answered with a loud voice, 'Why do you ask me regarding Jesus the Son of Man? He is now sitting in the heavens, on the right hand of great Power, and is about to come on the clouds of heaven.' And as many were confirmed, and gloried in this testimony of James, they said, Hosanna to the Son of David."[18]

It seems that the original Hebrew meaning of the word "Hosanna" faded over the years, especially in Greek-speaking churches. In his book, *Paedagogus* (The Instructor), Clement of Alexandria (150 – 215 AD) explains the meaning of "Hosanna" as follows:

> Light, and glory, and praise, with supplication to the Lord; for this is the meaning of the expression Hosanna.[19]

On this day, when the Church shouts "Hosanna," it is intending both meanings, that is pleading God for help to fulfil our salvation as well as praising and giving thanks to the One who became our salvation and redemption.[20]

Thus, the word "Hosanna" has become the most important liturgical prayer in the Coptic Church on this day, and it was used in the Responses to the Liturgy Gospels until very recently. It is also used in the liturgical prayer in the Byzantine Church all year long, as well as in the Latin Rite.

---

[18] Eusebius of Caesarea, *EH*, 2.23.
[19] *Theological Dictionary of the New Testament*, Volume IX, 683.
[20] Refer to the author's book on the *Dictionary of Ecclesiastical Terms*.

About the Hosanna Tune or the Hosanna Rite

We need to distinguish between the Hosanna tune or rite and the joyful tune or rite with which we pray on most of the Lordly feasts and during the Holy Fifty Days.

The Psali and the Verses of Cymbals are recited in the same way in both rites, that is the Hosanna and the Joyful ones. Both forms of chants are independent of the ecclesial occasion.

For example, the Psali tune is the same in the Annual Rite and Great Lent. Nevertheless, we cannot say that the Lenten Rite is identical to the Annual one. On the other hand, there are two possible tunes for the Verses of Cymbals, a greater one, which is dubbed the Joyful Tune, and a short one, which is called the Annual. The Verses of Cymbals could be chanted with the greater tune at any time of year, especially on feasts, while the short tune is more fitting for non-festal days, whether during the annual period, Koiak or Lent.

Hence, the tunes of the Psali and Verses of Cymbals tunes are not determined by the type or form of the rite itself.

The Joyful Rite has some distinct features that do not exist in the Hosanna Rite. First, the Joyful Rite includes a response for the Gospel Psalm which has no counterpart in the Hosanna Rite. Furthermore, the Joyful Rite includes special distribution hymns, while the Hosanna Rite does not.[21]

While the Joyful Rite is prayed in the joyful tune, the Hosanna Rite is prayed in the tune of the Cross, as is evidenced in all the contemporary Church Order manuscripts, as well as the ones undergoing study.

The Emergence of the Hosanna Procession and its Manifestations throughout the Ages

The prayers of this holy day begin in the evening of Lazarus Saturday when the Christians cut palms and olive branches[22] and adorn them with candles. The priests would approach the patriarch's or bishop's cell, wearing their priestly garments and carrying censers in their hands, accompanied by deacons holding candles and the children in innocence, chanting before him the Hosanna hymn until they reached the chorus. It seems

---

[21] I mention these facts due to some confusion that mixed up both rites. Refer to the book on *The Desire of the Souls in the Order of the Rites* (Coptic Orthodox Church Cantors Association, 1986), 58.

[22] It is an old tradition although the Gospels do not specifically state that they were olive branches. The gospels only record that they were tree branches. However, it is well known that the descent of the Mount of Olives, from which Christ's procession went up to Jerusalem, was filled with olive trees, hence the name of the mountain.

that the custom of greeting dignitaries with palms was well known even in Pharaonic Egypt.[23]

This Hosanna procession was known in the Middle Ages by the name "Olive Procession." During this ceremonial procession, the "Hosanna Hymn" is chanted. It is originally a Greek hymn with only the last two verses in Coptic:[24]

Blessed is He who comes in the name of the Lord; again in the name of the Lord.	Εὐλογημένος ὁ ἐρχόμενος ἐν ὀνόματι Κυρίου (Πάλιν) ἐν ὀνόματι Κυρίου.
Hosanna to the Son of David; again to the Son of David.	Ὡσαννὰ τῷ Υἱῷ Δαυείδ. (Πάλιν) τῷ Υἱῷ Δαυείδ.
Hosanna in the highest; again in the highest.	Ὡσαννὰ ἐν τοῖς ὑψίστοις. (Πάλιν) ἐν τοῖς ὑψίστοις.
Hosanna to the King of Israel; again to the King of Israel.	Ὡσαννὰ Βασιλεῖ τοῦ Ἰσραήλ. (Πάλιν) Βασιλεῖ τοῦ Ισραήλ.
Let us chant saying: Alleluia (3).	Τενερψαλιν ενχω ммос: Ἀλληλουϊά, ἀλληλουϊά, ἀλληλουϊά.
Glory be to our God; again glory be to our God.	Πι`ωογ φα πεννογϯ πε.

This hymn has two tunes, a long one, which is rarely used now but was common until the early part of the

---

[23] Morad Kamel, *The Coptic Era in the History of the Egyptian Civilization* (Cairo: 1963), 297.
[24] Oswald H.E. KHS-Burmester, "The Greek Kirugmata, Versicles and Responses, and Hymns in the Coptic Liturgy," *Orientalia Christiana Periodica II*, 3-4 (1936), 387.

seventies in the twentieth century, and a shorter one which is more common in churches today.

This hymn is chanted three times within the liturgical prayers of this feast, that is before Vespers, Matins and the Liturgy Gospel Readings.

The chant of "Blessed is He who comes in the name of the Lord (Benedictus qui venit in nominee Domini)" is also a common practice in Jerusalem during the ceremony of this day.[25]

On the other hand, the rite of bringing the patriarch or the bishop into the church in a procession[26] is a liturgical replication of what the crowd did when they brought Jesus in a procession to Jerusalem to enter the temple. Originally, it was performed as he entered the church before commencing the prayers of the Vespers Praise and Raising of Incense, as it was evening when Jesus entered the temple:

> And when he had looked round at everything, as it was already late, he went out to Bethany with the twelve. (Mark 11:11)

---

[25] Dom Emmanuel Lanne, *op. cit.*, 286.
[26] The "ceremonial procession" in the Coptic Tradition corresponds to the "Circling" in the Byzantian Church and the "March" in the Syriac Church.

The Spanish tourist, Egeria, who visited Jerusalem in the fourth century, was the first to speak of the Hosanna procession in its country of origin. She affirmed that this ceremonial procession had originated in Jerusalem and spread from there to the Eastern Churches.

The same is confirmed by the German scholar, Baumstark, in a quick note[27], as well as in the book of Church Readings of the Church of Georgia, "Le Lectionaire Géorgien."[28]

In her account of this procession, Egeria mentioned that the rites of this feast in the Church of Jerusalem imitate the triumphal entry of Christ and its relation to the Liturgy Service of this feast. The bishop, who resembles Christ, would ride on a colt, surrounded by the people, in a procession that began from the Eleona Church on the Mount of Olives in the afternoon of Lazarus Saturday. The people, especially the children, would carry palms and olive branches and cry out saying: "Hosanna! Blessed is He who comes in the name of the Lord." After the procession passed through the city streets, it would head to the Church of the Anastasis (Resurrection), where they would perform the prayers and praises at the dawn of Sunday, followed by the service of the Holy Liturgy.

---

[27] Anton Baumstark, Das Leydener, 48-49.
[28] Dom Emmanuel Lanne, *op. cit.*, 286.

Hence, we can see that the Hosanna procession in Jerusalem was celebrated in the afternoon, and that they would reach the Church of Golgotha by the beginning of the night after the procession had descended from the Mount of Olives.[29] In the same manner, the original Hosanna procession and the Lord's entry into Jerusalem lasted all of Sunday, so that they reached the temple at the end of the procession, and when He looked round at everything, as it was already late, he went out to stay in Bethany.

The same rite was practiced by the Coptic Church until the twelfth century, as the Hosanna procession would roam around the cities and villages at the eve of the feast of Palm Sunday. It was customary for Copts to raise the Cross in the streets with readings and hymns through the night. This is confirmed in the book of the *History of the Patriarchs of the Egyptian Church* in the beginning of the eleventh century, where we read the following:

---

[29] Egeria described that the celebration of Palm Sunday in Jerusalem in the fourth century was as follows: the congregation gathers at dawn in the Church of Resurrection; from there they relocate to the Church of Golgotha where they pray the usual Sunday Service. Then, in the early afternoon, they move to the Mount of Olives, where they perform another service. Around three in the afternoon, they transfer to the place of Christ's ascension, where they perform yet another service. Around five in the afternoon, they go back to Jerusalem, carrying palms and olive branches, and pray the sunset prayer in the Church of Resurrection. From there, they return to the Church of Golgotha and conclude the day with some final prayers.

It was a custom for the Christians of Alexandria to go out with olive branches on the day of the Feast of Olive Branches, on the eve, and to pass with them through the main street and the market from the Church of Saint Abba Sergius to the Church of the Saviour with intercession and reading, until something happened on the part of Muslims which obliged them (the Christians) to remain fifteen years without conducting procession with them (the branches). When we mentioned this to the Amir Hisn Al-Dawlah Ibn Mirua, he ordered (us) to go out with them (the olive branches) according to the usual custom, and he sent with us his companions and instructed them to do what he told them. From whatsoever house a stone was thrown a seal should be placed on its door, and he should be informed about it, and whatsoever man of the Muslims should speak (against us), should be taken to prison. His public herald proclaimed this in the city, so we took them (the olive branches) out that night, and we went in procession with them through the city with reading and laudation, and crosses and incense, as it had been the custom before. It was for us a good night, and this was in the year four hundred and four of the Khiragyah[30]... Abundance increased, and God in His mercy and His compassion lifted our dearth. The Muslim inhabitants of Alexandria were certain that this was through the blessing of bringing out olive branches and carrying them in procession through the city, and they used to rejoice at the going out with them every year on the eve of the Feast of Olive Branches up until now...[31]

---

[30] That is the year 404 AH which corresponds to the year 1013 AD.
[31] History of the Patriarchs of the Egyptian Church: Severus Ibn Al-Muqaffa' of Al-Ashmūnīn, *History of the Holy Church*, Vol. 2, Volume 3, edited by Yassā 'abd Al-Masīḥ, Aziz Soriel 'ateya, and

The German scholar, A. Baumstark, also mentions this custom, which was performed in Egypt especially in the countryside, where Christ was represented with a cross in the Palm Sunday procession. He says:

> In Egypt, Christ was represented by the Cross which was carried in triumph in the villages and countryside in celebration of this occasion.[32]

However, this custom ceased in Egypt in the second half of the twelfth century during the days of Pope Mark III, the 73rd Patriarch of Alexandria (1166 – 1189 AD).

This explains why in the Byzantine Rite the Christians adorned the palms and the olive branches with candles. It also clarifies why in the Byzantine Rite of the eleventh and twelfth centuries lighted candles were carried as well as the palms in the ceremonial procession of this day.[33]

On the other hand, the Procession of Palm Sunday and the Blessing of Palms was known in the Latin Church at a much later era, as no trace of these ceremonies was found in the first thousand years, that is, before the

---

Oswald H.E. KHS-Burmester (Cairo: Publications de la Société d'Archéologie Copte, 1959), 179-180.
[32] Anton Baumstark, Bernard Botte and F L Cross, *Comparative Liturgy* (London: A.R. Mowbray, 1958), 149.
[33] *Ibid.*, 149.

ascendancy of the Imperial German power. By contrast, the Procession of Palm Sunday was celebrated earlier in Carolingian France, perhaps during the eighth or ninth century.

The Greek Typikon of the Holy City informs us of the text of the hymns and prayers which were in use over the following five or six centuries. Between the years 496 and 502 AD, the Chatholicos Babbi introduced the Ceremony of Palms into the Persian Church, which were later adopted by the Nestorian/Assyrian Church. During the same period, Edessa received this rite. On the other hand, pre-Islamic Arabic poetries indicate that it was admitted at Al-Hira, the capital of the Lakhmids. The rite then spread to Spain at the time of St. Isidore of Seville (560 – 636 AD).[34] Furthermore, it has become so popular in the Antiochian Church that a document going back to 834 AD introduces it as one of the greatest ecclesiastical celebrations in which the entire populations of towns and villages assembled to participate.[35] Currently, the Byzantine Church celebrates the Hosanna Procession after the service of the Holy Liturgy.

Nowadays, the Hosanna Procession has been relegated to the prayers of the Matins Raising of Incense on Palm

---

[34] *ODCC*, 2nd edition, 717.
[35] Anton Baumstark, *op. cit.*, 148.

Sunday, which I will go on to explain later in its due place.

Chapter Two: The Rites of Vespers Praise and Raising of Incense Prayers of Palm Sunday

First: Vespers Praise of Palm Sunday

1. According to the Manuscripts and the Old Liturgical References

(a) By Ibn Kabar

In the *Manuscript of Paris*:

> The prayer is held in the evening of Lazarus Saturday, the Hymns of the Cross are chanted, and the Commentary of the same feast is read, which goes: Μαϣενακ ϩιϫεν ογτωογ εϥϭοϲι.

In the *Manuscript of Uppsala*:

> The prayer is held in the evening of Lazarus Saturday[1], the Theotokion is read with its hymns (if possible), and the Lobsh/Explanation is chanted with the tune of the Feast of the Cross, followed by the Commentary, which reads Μαϣενακ ϩιϫεν ογ. They continue the prayer and read the canon[2] specific for this day,[3] which reads Ραϣι ογνοϥ Ϲιων ϯβακι.

---

[1] Manuscript of the Patriarchate: + as usual.
[2] That is the Concluding Prayer.
[3] The term "specific for this day" is not mentioned in the *Vatican Manuscript*.

(b) In the Manuscripts under study

The *Manuscript of the Roman Quarter Typikon (15th century)* includes a Batos Psali, titled "Batos Psali for Palm Sunday and the Entry of our Saviour into Jerusalem," written entirely in Coptic only. It starts as follows: ⲁⲙⲱⲓⲛⲓ ⲧⲏⲣⲟⲩ ⲱ ⲛⲓⲡⲓⲥⲧⲟⲥ ⲛⲧⲉⲛϯ ⲱⲟⲩ ⲛⲓⲏⲥ Ⲡⲭⲥ..., which translates to:

> O come all you believers, let us glorify Jesus Christ with the children of the Hebrews saying: Hosanna in the highest...

According to *The Typikon and Order of the Passion Week and the Glorious Passover Feast (1920)* (p. 57), this Psali is said before the Commemoration in the Midnight Praise of Palm Sunday.[4]

In addition, the manuscript includes an "Adam Psali for Palm Sunday" that is acrostically arranged after the Coptic alphabet. It starts as follows: ⲁⲣⲓⲥⲁⲗⲡⲓⲍⲓⲛ ⲙⲫⲟⲟⲩ: ϧⲉⲛ ⲛⲉⲧⲉⲛϣⲁⲓ: ⲟⲩⲟϩ ⲁⲣⲓⲯⲁⲗⲓⲛ: ϧⲉⲛ ⲡϣⲁⲓ ⲛⲁⲁⲱⲛⲁⲓ, which translates to: "Blow the trumpet today in your feast and sing on the feast of the Son of God." This Psali was written by Nicodemus. Although he does not

---

[4] I will include its entire script later on.

mention his name, it follows his style, for in the final three verses, he writes:

> Grant us to see Jerusalem, the place of Your tomb, Zion and Bethlehem, the Resurrection, the land of the Jordan, the Mount of Kranion, 'the tomb of the mother of God', and the tomb of the righteous Lazarus.

On the other hand, the *Manuscript of Abba Shenoute Typikon (14th century)* states:

> On the night of Palm Sunday, the psalms are read as usual, followed by this Psali. And glory be to our God.

It then discloses the Adam Psali of Palm Sunday in both Coptic and Arabic,[5] but is ordered after the Coptic alphabet. It starts as follows:

> Blow the trumpet at the New Moon and sing today in your feasts. Loosen from your hearts the evil thoughts for the merciful Lord rides on a colt.

The manuscript, then, goes on to say:

---

[5] It is the same Psali that came in *The 1920 Guide and Order of the Passion Week and the Glorious Passover Feast*, that is the Adam Psali said before the First Canticle.

The Theotokion and the Hails are then read in the Tune of the Cross of the Cross, followed by the Commentary and `Ⲱ ⲡⲉⲛⲟⲥ Ihc Ⲡⲭⲥ.

The *Manuscript of the Hanging Church Typikon* states:

> They start the Vespers Prayer as usual until the end of ` ⲤⲘⲞⲨ ` ⲈⲠⲞⲤ ` ⲈⲂⲞⲖ.[6] Then the following Batos Psali[7] is read, followed by the Theotokion and the *Hails* in the Tune of the Cross, then the Commentary, `Ⲱ Ⲡⲉⲛⲟⲥ Ihc Ⲡⲭⲥ, and they raise incense as usual...[8]

(c) In the Church Order Manuscripts

The *Church Order Manuscript No. 118 (Rites) in Cairo Patriarchate for the year 1911* states the following:[9]

---

[6] This is the Fourth Canticle.
[7] The manuscript includes the Psali in Coptic only, which is the same as the directly aforementioned one.
[8] The same is mentioned in the *Manuscript of the Hanging Church Typikon (16th century)* as well as in the *Manuscript of Haret Zuweila Typikon (17th century)*.
[9] The text is included here after correcting the typos and grammatical errors. The exact same text also came in the *Church Order Manuscript No. 73 (Rites) in Cairo Patriarchate for the year 1444*, the *Manuscript of Al-Baramūs Monastery 1514*, and the *Manuscript of the Syrian Monastery 1698*.

If the patriarch or the bishop is present, they go up[10] to him with candles and cymbals and bring him to the church while chanting Ⲉⲩⲗⲟⲅⲏⲙⲉⲛⲟⲥ [11] until they reach the chorus. They start the prayer with reading the psalms as usual until the end of ⸀Ⲥⲙⲟⲩ ⸀ⲉⲡⲟⲥ.[12] Then they say the Batos Psali of Palm Sunday,[13] followed by the Theotokion. The *Hails (Sherat)* are chanted in the Tune of the Cross, the Commentary is also read in tune, and afterwards they say ⸀ Ⲱ ⲡⲉⲛⲟⲥ.[14]

2. Commentary and Explanation of the Vespers Praise Rite of Palm Sunday

The Patriarch's or the Bishop's Procession into the Church

The Church Rite, as described in the Church Order manuscripts, dictates that the patriarch or the bishop goes to the church before the Vespers Praise. The following is a description of the liturgical elements of Palm Sunday Vespers Praise.

---

[10] The tense of this verb is corrected, along with the other like verbs.
[11] This is the Hosanna Tune (Evlogimenos), but the manuscript only mentions it in Coptic.
[12] This is till the end of the Fourth Canticle.
[13] I will include its script later on.
[14] This is currently known as the Theotokia Batos Conclusion.

Yoḥanna Ibn Abī Zakaria Ibn Sebā'[15] mentions the following in his book, *The Precious Jewel in Church Sciences (Ketāb al-Jawhara al-Nafīsa fī 'Oloum al-Kanīsa)*, about the entry of the patriarch or the bishop into the church on the eve of Palm Sunday:

> ... therefore, the Christians ought to celebrate in this holy manner every year by cutting palms and olive branches on Lazarus Saturday, weaving them into one big honourable olive branch with crosses and candles implanted in it, and carrying it to the Patriarchal cell.[16]

While the Church Order manuscripts indicate that they escort the patriarch or bishop to the church with candles and cymbals, *The Typikon and Order of the Passion Week and the Glorious Passover Feast (1920)* adds that they bring him up with palms and olive branches. The latter reads:[17]

---

[15] From my many readings of Yoḥanna Ibn Sebā' and Shams Al-Ri'āsa Ibn Kabar, it seems that Ibn Sebā' preceded Ibn Kabar in time. Since the latter lived in the second half of the thirteenth century till the first quarter of the fourteenth century, then Ibn Sebā' may have lived in the first half of the thirteenth century or a bit earlier than that. It is also possible that he lived in Upper Egypt during the time of Ibn Kabar. In either case, his testimony about the Coptic Church Rites is extremely important.

[16] Yoḥanna Ibn Abī Zakaria Ibn Sebā', *The Precious Jewel in Church Sciences (Ketāb al-Jawhara al-Nafīsa fī 'Oloum al-Kanīsa)*, op. cit., 318.

[17] This is written in bold font, which adds significance, but it was not mentioned in the Church Order manuscripts.

> In the evening of Lazarus Saturday, all the Christians start to cut palms and olive branches and weave them in the shape of a cross, lighting them up with candles. They, then, go up to the cell of the patriarch, the Metropolitan, or the bishop, along with the priests wearing their priestly garments and having censers in their hands and the deacons holding up candles in their hands, and they chant Ⲉⲩⲗⲟⲅⲏⲙⲉⲛⲟⲥ before him in the Hosanna Tune until they reach the chorus. They start with the prayers of the Ninth, Eleventh and Twelfth Hours and the Veil. Afterwards, they say Ⲛⲓⲉⲑⲛⲟⲥ, followed by the Fourth Canticle…[18]

From the biography of Abba Peter V (1340 – 1348 AD), the 83rd Patriarch of Alexandria, we read the following account when he prepared the Holy Chrism in the Monastery of St. Macarius in the year 1340:

> … and in the eve of this day, the eve of Palm Sunday, the pope came down from his cell, along with the bishops and those who were with him. They began with the Vespers Prayer of Palm Sunday and reached the Theotokia, of which some were intoned and some were not. Anba Gabriel, the Bishop of Taha, read the Commentary, while Anba Mark, the Bishop of Al-Behera, concluded the prayer. They, then, continued the prayer of Sunday Eve as usual.[19]

---

[18] *The 1920 Guide and Order of the Passion Week and the Glorious Passover Feast*, 17.

[19] Manuscript No. 100 (Arabic) at the National Library in Paris.

Psali of Palm Sunday

This Batos Psali, referred to in all ancient liturgical references and in most manuscripts under study, is the first prayer encountered on this holy day – a truly magnificent Psali in meaning and structure.

Ibn Kabar (1324 AD) mentions that it is chanted with the tune of the Cross in the Vespers of Palm Sunday. The Church Order manuscripts also point out that the Cross/Hosanna Tune is used on Palm Sunday to pray the *Hails (Sherat)*, as well as the Exposition. The same can also be found in the *Manuscript of the Hanging Church Typikon*.

On the other hand, *The Typikon and Order of the Passion Week and the Glorious Passover Feast (1920)* refers to the tune of this Psali, saying: "and this Batos Psali uses the Joyful Tune," which is not mentioned elsewhere.

The following is the full text of the Psali:
- Blow at the new moon with the sound trumpet on your feast day for God command it.
- Loosen from your hearts the evil thoughts, envy and ignorance, and every guile and malice.
- O you believers, celebrate an angelic feast with psalms and praises and spiritual songs.
- Songs of David saying, "Blessed is He who comes in the name of the good Lord, from now and to the end of time."

- Let the fields rejoice and everyone on them for the Coming of Christ our God according to the prophetic voices.
- The pure Zechariah by the Holy Spirit likewise said, "Rejoice O daughter of Zion.
- Behold your King is coming in glory and honour and with good hymns, riding on a donkey."
- Isaiah, the worshiper of God, spoke with the divine voice, with a good and clever tongue, "Tell the cities of Judah.
- Behold your majestic Lord comes like a shepherd who shepherds his flock and comforts them."
- And also our father Jacob said, "The authority will not leave Judah until the Coming of Him who has the power of many tongues."
- Every nation and the tribes wait upon Him to tie His colt to the vine in joy.
- Let us all say with Jeremiah the good prophet, "This is our God, and we know no one but Him."
- He found every way of knowledge and granted it to Jacob with understanding and to Israel as they deserve.
- Suddenly thereafter He appeared on earth and participated in walking with the people of the earth.
- A wonder full of glory, He who sits upon the Cherubim on this day entered Jerusalem.
- The King and the Creator, the Unseen One, was seen riding a donkey, and the children before Him.
- Chanting fervently in good voices, praising His greatness without silence.
- Praising diligently saying, "This is Emmanuel, hosanna in the highest, this is the King of Israel."
- Then He perfected the sayings of David the spirit-mantled, "Out of the mouths of nursing infants You have prepared praise."

- Therefore, the Hebrews took palms and olives and their garments and spread them before Him on the road.
- On which He walked upon, saying "This is truly He who is anticipated as the Sun of righteousness."
- Holy Holy Holy, we praise You as believers with the children a hundred-fold and worship Your divinity.
- O Saviour of the world, the beloved Son of God, we proclaim saying, "Hosanna to the Son of David."
- Hosanna in the highest, grant us grace and mercy on Judgment Day, and have mercy on us according to Your great mercy.

The first verse of this Psali, taken from the third verse of Psalm 80,[20] is repeated five times over the course of the prayers of this feast.[21] This practice is quite remarkable, and thus we shall trace its origins.

The third verse of Psalm 80 confirms that it was recited as a communal prayer in celebration of the feast. In fact, the first five verses of the Psalm are considered a call for worship on this feast, which is probably the "Feast of Tabernacles."[22]

---

[20] This is Psalm 81 in the Beirut Translation.
[21] It is recited a second time in the Adam Psali, which is prayed on the First Canticle in the Midnight Praise; a third time in the Adam Psali, which is prayed on the Third Canticle; a fourth time in the first verse of the Doxology of Palm Sunday; and a fifth time in the Psalm of the Liturgy Gospel.
[22] According to the New Oxford Annotated Bible. We also read this in Deuteronomy 16:13-15.

This feast, mentioned in the Psalm, is also called the "Feast of Ingathering" as it came towards the end of the year when the crops are gathered from the field.[23] It is one of the major feasts on which every male Israelite is committed to celebrate for the Lord in Jerusalem. The three major feasts are:
- Feast of Passover, or Unleavened Bread (Exodus 23:14)
- Feast of Harvest (Exodus 34:22), or Feast of Weeks (Exodus 23:22), or Feast of Firstfruits (Numbers 28:26), or Feast of Pentecost (Acts 2:1)
- Feast of Ingathering (Exodus 34:22), or Feast of Tabernacles (Deuteronomy 16:13), which is called in the New Testament "the Great Feast," while the Jews also call it "Hoshana Rabbah" that is "the Great Hosanna."

The Israelites celebrate the Feast of Tabernacles on the fifteenth of the seventh month for a period of seven days. On the first day, they rejoice before the Lord with branches of palms trees, boughs of leafy trees, and willows of the brook, while dwelling in tents.[24] After the construction of the temple, they set up the tents in the squares of Jerusalem, on the rooftops and courtyards of

---

[23] Exodus 23:16
[24] Refer to Leviticus 23:39-44

houses, in the courts of the temple,[25] and on the mountains around Jerusalem in commemoration of their dwelling in tents in the wilderness after their exodus from the land of Egypt. Some grand ceremonies were later added to the ones commanded by the Law.

The people would gather in the temple in the early morning; and at the time of the morning sacrifice, they enter the court of the temple carrying branches of palm trees and woven branches of myrtle and willow. They circle around the brazen altar once every day, and seven times on the seventh day, as testified by Josephus the historian.[26]

One of the priests fills a golden jar with water from the Pool of Siloam at the base of Mount Zion, and with great awe scoops water three times. He, then, returns with the golden jar to the sanctuary in a triumphal procession, passing through the Water Gate. When he enters the temple, he is received with the sound of trumpets and continuous joyful tunes until he arrived at the highest level of the altar.

---

[25] Nehemiah 8:16
[26] Refer to 2 Maccabees 10:6-7

While he pours water on the altar, the entire congregation would recite the words of Isaiah the prophet, "With joy you will draw water from the wells of salvation" (Isaiah 12:3). Then, they chant the Psalms of Gladness[27], followed by the Great Praise that is Psalm 136.[28] When they reach the verse that says, "O give thanks to the Lord, for He is good, for His mercy endures for ever," they would wave the palms and branches in their hands.

Jesus Christ referred to Himself in terms of this ritual, proclaiming Himself as the living water saying, "If any one thirst, let him come to me and drink. He who believes in me, as the scripture has said, 'Out of his heart shall flow rivers of living water'" (John 7:37-38).

Consequently, it is fitting that Psalm 80 would take a pre-eminent place in this feast, for it is not instituted by man but by the order of God, as the words of the Psalm show. Thus, the Church goes forth in its lively path replacing the symbol with the truth, for the former finds its very purpose when it leads to the latter.

---

[27] These are Psalms 113-118
[28] Psalm 136 in Hebrew is Psalm 135 in the Septuagint and the Second Canticle in the Coptic Midnight Praise.

The Commentary of Palm Sunday
After praying the Theotokia and the *Hails (Sherat)* with the Tune of the Cross, the Introduction of the Commentary is also prayed in the same tune, followed by the reading of the Commentary. Thus, the Commentary is read at the end of the Vespers Praise as is common during the entire liturgical year. This is mentioned by Ibn Kabar (1324 AD), as well as the Church Order manuscripts, and the other manuscripts under study.

However, *The Typikon and Order of the Passion Week and the Glorious Passover Feast (1920)* specifies that the Commentary is read during the prayers of the Vespers Raising of Incense, before the Litany of the Gospel[29] and after the Hosanna Hymn which follows the priest's Ⲫϯ ⲚⲀⲒ ⲚⲀⲚ.

The Commentary of Palm Sunday is a very old one and is known by its first Coptic word Ⲙⲁϣⲉⲛⲁⲕ (Mashenak) that is "ascend." It is based on the Book of Isaiah and nine verses from the Gospel Reading according to St. Matthew which is read during the Liturgy Service of the Feast.

---

[29] *The Guide and Order of the Passion Week and the Glorious Passover Feast* (1920), 23.

The entire text of the Commentary is kept to date in the Northern (Bohairic) Coptic dialect, but I also found the first three verses only in the Southern (Sahidic) Coptic dialect in Volume 14 of the Pierpont Morgan manuscripts, which goes back to the ninth century AD, more specifically to the year 609 AM / 892-893 AD.[30]

The following is the text of the Commentary as it came in the Northern (Bohairic) Coptic dialect, along with the minor differences between both dialects over the first three verses.

The Text
- Ascend to the high mountains[31] O annunciator of Zion. Raise your voice with strength and preach to Jerusalem.
- Tell the cities ("Proclaim amongst the cities") of Judah: Behold, your King comes ("is coming to you") with His wage, and His deeds are before Him ("with His winnowing fork in His hands, and He will clear His field").
- Like a shepherd who shepherds his flock and with his high hands ("mighty staff") gathers the lambs.
- Arise and adorn your gates for the Son of the God is coming to save you with purity and peace.

---

[30] Oswald H.E. KHS-Burmester, *The Turuhat of the Coptic Church*, OCP, III (1937), 81-82.
[31] It came by Ibn Kabar as: Ascend to the high mountain. Cf. Oswald H.E. KHS-Burmester, *The Turuhat of the Coptic Church*, *op. cit.*, 90.

- Behold, all your children will come to Him rejoicing, while proclaiming and saying, "Hosanna to the Son of David."
- ...[32]
- Oh, how great is this wonder: He who sits upon the Cherubim rode on a colt of a donkey according to the Economy.
- He is on the earth and has never left the heavens. He sits in the bosom of His Father and is present in Jerusalem.
- The children of the Hebrews spread their garments before Him, and the Cherubim were covering their faces with their wings.
- They were worthily glorifying with unceasing lips, saying, "Blessed is the glory of Lord in Salmon, His holy mountain."
- They were praising and saying: "Hosanna to the Son of David." Blessed is the Lord Jesus Christ who came to save us.

There is another Commentary that is only mentioned in *The Typikon and Order of the Passion Week and the Glorious Passover Feast (1920)*, which is titled "And also." It is made up of twelve verses and is written in the Northern (Bohairic) Coptic dialect. It is based on verses 12-15 from the Gospel Reading according to St. John which is read during the Liturgy Service of the Feast.[33]

---

[32] There are six verses here that summarise the events in the Gospel when Jesus sent two of His disciples to bring Him a colt to ride on when He enters Jerusalem.
[33] John 12:12-19.

I have found only two verses of this Commentary, that is verses four and five, in the Southern (Sahidic) Coptic dialect in the Pierpont Morgan manuscripts.

This Commentary starts with the following verses in the Northern (Bohairic) Coptic dialect. I will also include the differences between both dialects in the text:[34]
- When Jesus drew near the descent of Mount Olives, ascending to Jerusalem,
- all the disciples began to rejoice and praise for all the mighty works they had seen,
- proclaiming and saying: "Hosanna to the Son of David. Hosanna in the highest. This is the King of Israel."
- But ("But" was not mentioned in the Southern (Sahidic) Coptic dialect) the next day, when the great multitude that had come ("had ascended") to the feast heard that Jesus was coming to Jerusalem,
- they took branches ("of palm trees") in their hands ("in their hands" was not mentioned in the Southern (Sahidic) Coptic dialect) and came out to meet Him and proclaimed, saying, "Hosanna to the Son of David (+ "This is the King of Israel")" ...

Thus, it is obvious that the first Commentary was particularly known in Church before the ninth

---

[34] Oswald H.E. KHS-Burmester, *The Turuhat of the Coptic Church*, op. cit., 82-83.

century, as it was mentioned in the manuscripts that go back to that century. This is quite ancient from the perspective of liturgical history, especially since most of our Coptic liturgical references are confined to the thirteenth and fourteenth century. Only the rarest of references extend before this period. This also explains why Ibn Kabar (1324 AD) only mentioned the first Commentary of "Ascend to the high mountains O annunciator of Zion..." in the rites of the Vespers of Palm Sunday, which implies that it is the oldest liturgical element of this great feast.

In accordance with the manuscripts, after reading the Commentary, the Batos Conclusion of the Theotokia is read, which concludes the prayers of the Vespers Praise of Palm Sunday.

Second: Vespers Raising of Incense Prayers of Palm Sunday

1. According to the Manuscripts and the Old Liturgical References

(a) By Ibn Kabar
In the *Manuscript of Uppsala*: "... they continue the prayer and read the canon specific for this day[35] Ⲣⲁϣⲓ ⲟⲩⲛⲟϥ Ⲥⲓⲱⲛ ϯⲃⲁⲕⲓ," which is the same as the aforementioned.

(b) In the Manuscripts under study
The *Manuscript of the Roman Quarter Typikon (15th century)* includes two Batos Doxologies that are prayed on the eve of Palm Sunday, one in the Vespers and another in the Matins. The former starts with Ⲁⲁⲅⲓⲁ ⲅⲁⲣ ⲡⲓⲓⲉⲣⲟⲯⲁⲗⲧⲏⲥ, but it does not exist in the Psalmody Book. The latter, on the other hand, is the first Doxology in the published Psalmody Book, and it starts with ⲁⲣⲓⲥⲁⲗⲡⲓⲍⲓⲛ ϧⲉⲛ ⲟⲩⲥⲟⲩⲁⲓ.

---

[35] The term "specific for this day" is not mentioned in the *Vatican Manuscript*.

The following is the text of this Batos Doxology that is mentioned by the stated manuscript but not in the published Psalmody Book.

For David the psalmist, the king of Israel, is joyfully praising in our midst, with doxologies of blessing.	Ⲇⲁⲩⲓⲇ ⲅⲁⲣ ⲡⲓⲓⲉⲣⲟⲯⲁⲗⲧⲏⲥ : ⲟⲩⲟϩ `ⲡⲟⲩⲣⲟ `ⲙⲡⲓⲥⲗ̅ : ⲉϥⲉⲣⲭⲟⲣⲉⲩⲥⲉ ϧⲉⲛ ⲧⲉⲛⲙⲏϯ : ϧⲉⲛ ϩⲁⲛⲇⲟⲝⲟⲗⲟⲅⲓⲁ `ⲛ`ⲥⲙⲟⲩ .
For out of the mouths of babes and nursing infants, You have perfected praise, as they bless Your Lordship.	Ϫⲉ `ⲉⲃⲟⲗϧⲉⲛ ⲣⲱⲟⲩ `ⲛϩⲁⲛⲕⲟⲩϫⲓ : `ⲛⲁⲗⲱⲟⲩ`ⲓ ⲛⲉⲙ ⲛⲓⲉⲑⲟⲩⲉⲙϭⲓ³⁶@ `ⲛⲑⲟⲕ ⲁⲕⲥⲉⲃⲧⲉ ⲡⲓ`ⲥⲙⲟⲩ : ⲉⲩⲉⲣϩⲩⲙⲛⲟⲥ ` ⲉⲧⲉⲕⲙⲉⲧⲥ̅ .
The heavenly hosts praise Him, proclaiming and saying: Hosanna in the highest, this is the King of Israel.	Ⲉⲩϩⲱⲥ `ⲉⲣⲟϥ `ⲛϫⲉ ⲛⲁ `ⲧⲫⲉ : ⲉⲩⲱϣ `ⲉⲃⲟⲗ ⲉⲩϫⲱ `ⲙⲙⲟⲥ : ϫⲉ `ⲱⲥⲁⲛⲛⲁ ϧⲉⲛ ⲛⲏⲉⲧϭⲟⲥⲓ : ⲫⲁⲓ ⲡⲉ `ⲡⲟⲩⲣⲟ `ⲙⲡⲓⲥⲗ̅ .
Bring to the Lord, O sons of God, bring to the Lord young rams. Bring to the Lord glory and honour. Bring glory to His name.	ⲁⲛⲓⲟⲩ`ⲓ Ⲡⲥ̅³⁷ `ⲛⲛⲓϣⲏⲣⲓ `ⲛⲧⲉ Ⲫϯ: ⲁⲛⲓⲟⲩ`ⲓ Ⲡⲥ̅ `ⲛϩⲁⲛϣⲏⲣⲓ ` ⲛⲱⲓⲗⲓ: ⲁⲛⲓⲟⲩ`ⲓ Ⲡⲥ̅ `ⲛⲟⲩ`ⲱⲟⲩ ⲛⲉⲙ ⲟⲩⲧⲁⲓⲟ : ⲁⲛⲓⲟⲩ`ⲓ `ⲛⲟⲩ` ⲱⲟⲩ `ⲙⲡⲉϥⲣⲁⲛ.
Worship Him in Jerusalem. Come and rejoice today. Let us rejoice in our Lord	Ⲟⲩⲱϣⲧ ⲛⲁϥ ϧⲉⲛ Ⲓⲗ̅ⲏ̅ⲙ̅ : ⲁⲙⲱⲓⲛⲓ ⲙⲁⲣⲉⲛⲑⲉⲗⲏⲗ `ⲙⲫⲟⲟⲩ : `ⲛⲧⲉⲛ-

---

³⁶ It came as ⲉⲑⲟⲩⲉⲙϣⲓ in the manuscript, but the correct is ⲉⲑⲟⲩⲉⲙϭⲓ.
³⁷ It came as Ⲡⲥ̅ in the manuscript, but correct is `ⲙⲠⲥ̅.

with doxologies of blessing. Saying: Hosanna to the Son of David, Hosanna in the highest. Blessed is the Lord of hosts.	ʼⲉϣⲏⲗⲟⲩʼⲓ ʼⲙⲡⲉⲛⲛⲟⲩϯ : ϧⲉⲛ ϩⲁⲛⲇⲟⲝⲟⲗⲟⲅⲓⲁ ʼⲛʼⲥⲙⲟⲩ. ϫⲉ ʼⲱⲥⲁⲛⲛⲁ ʼⲡϣⲏⲣⲓ ʼⲛⲇⲁⲩⲓⲇ : ʼⲱⲥⲁⲛⲛⲁ ϧⲉⲛ ⲛⲏⲉⲧϭⲟⲥⲓ : ʼϥʼ ⲥⲙⲁⲣⲱⲟⲩⲧ Ⲡ̄ⲟ̄ⲥ̄ ʼⲛⲧⲉ ⲛⲓϫⲟⲙ.

As for the Vespers Gospel Response, it is quite familiar to us, and starts with Ⲭⲉⲣⲉ ⲗⲁⲍⲁⲣⲟⲥ, "Hail to Lazarus whom You raised[38]..."

At the time of reading the Adam Commentary, they chant the Feast Hymn of Ⲉⲩⲗⲟⲅⲏⲙⲉⲛⲟⲥ.

With respect to the Concluding Prayer, the manuscript indicates: "They lift the Cross and say the canon," which starts with Ⲣⲁϣⲓ ⲟⲩⲛⲟϥ Ⲥⲓⲱⲛ, "Rejoice and be glad O city of Zion..."

The *Manuscript of Abba Shenoute Typikon (14th century)* states the following:

> The Raising of Incense is prayed as usual until the end of the Gospel Reading when they respond with this verse Ⲭⲉⲣⲉ ⲗⲁⲍⲁⲣⲟⲥ. Then they continue the prayer as usual. Afterwards, they light candles and proceed to the icon of Palm Sunday while chanting the hymn of Ⲉⲩⲗⲟⲅⲏⲙⲉⲛⲟⲥ as is customary

---

[38] Not "whom He raised" as it came in the manuscript.

in the Hanging Church, while in some[39] places they first say ⸀ Ⲕ⸀ⲥⲙⲁⲣⲱⲟⲩⲧ with the Tune of the Cross of the Cross. They read the Commentary in Coptic and Arabic until the end of Ⲙⲁϣⲉⲛⲁⲕ... They then raise the Gospel and Cross and pray Kyrie eleison. As the congregation kisses them, they recite this canon with the Tune of Paul, Ⲣⲁϣⲓ ⲟⲩⲛⲟϥ Ⲥⲓⲱⲛ ϯⲃⲁⲕⲓ.[40]

The *Manuscript of the Hanging Church Typikon* states:

> They raise incense as usual and respond to the Gospel with this response which was written first Ⲭⲉⲣⲉ ⲗⲁⲍⲁⲣⲟⲥ, then continue the prayer as usual. After the Absolution of the Son, they chant the Hosanna Hymn Ⲉⲩⲗⲟⲅⲏⲙⲉⲛⲟⲥ[41] while proceeding to the icon of Palm Sunday with lit candles in their hands. Then, they say this verse with the Tune of the Cross, Ⲱⲥⲁⲛⲛⲁ ϧⲉⲛ ⲛⲏⲉⲧϭⲟⲥⲓ. Afterwards, they chant the Commentary with the Tune of the Cross, as with the entire procession, Ⲙⲁϣⲉⲛⲁⲕ ϩⲓϫⲉⲛ ⲛⲟⲩⲧⲱⲟⲩ...[42] and then read it in Arabic, followed by ⸀Ⲡⲟⲩⲣⲟ ⸀ⲛⲧⲉ ϯϩⲓⲣⲏⲛⲏ. At the end, they raise the Gospel and the Cross and pray Kyrie eleison. Then, the congregation kisses them[43] while the deacons chant this canon in the Tune of Paul, Ⲣⲁϣⲓ ⲟⲩⲛⲟϥ

---

[39] The word "some" is misspelled in the manuscript.
[40] The manuscript includes the full text of the canon in both Coptic and Arabic.
[41] The manuscript includes the full text of the hymn in Coptic only.
[42] That is "Ascend to the high mountains O annunciator of Zion..." The manuscript includes the full text in both Coptic and Arabic.
[43] In the manuscript: "the congregation accepts them"

Ⲥⲓⲱⲛ ϯⲃⲁⲕⲓ.[44] They then conclude the prayer with the benediction, and the congregation rests for a while before commencing the Midnight Prayer as usual…[45]

On the other hand, after the statement "This concludes what is to be read on Lazarus Saturday. Praise be to God." in the *Manuscript of London Typikon*, it states immediately afterwards what indicates that some pages are missing from the manuscript, as we read the following in the beginning of the page:

…while they are in the chorus. When they reach the first Hosanna, with candles in their hands, they proceed to the icon of Palm Sunday and continue the rest of the Hymn. The Hosanna is chanted in the Tune of the Cross and then read it in Arabic. They say `Ⲡⲟⲩⲣⲟ `ⲛⲧⲉ ϯϩⲓⲣⲏⲛⲏ, and then raise the Bible and the cross and recite the canon of Ⲡⲁϣⲓ ⲟⲩⲛⲟϥ Ⲥⲓⲱⲛ ϯⲃⲁⲕⲓ. The prayer is then concluded with the benediction. They rest for a while and then start the Midnight Prayer as usual …

(c) The Church Order Manuscript No. 118 (Rites) at the Patriarchate

---

[44] The manuscript includes the full text in Coptic only.
[45] The same is mentioned by the *Manuscript of the Hanging Church Typikon (16th century)* and the *Manuscript of Haret Zuweila Typikon (17th century)*.

They raise incense as usual[46] and say ⲁⲣⲓⲕⲁⲧⲁⲍⲓⲟⲓⲛ.[47] Then they pray the Batos Doxology of Palm Sunday, that is ⲁⲣⲓⲥⲁⲗⲡⲓⲍⲓⲛ ϧⲉⲛ ⲟⲩⲥⲟⲩⲁⲓ...,[48] and also if they chose to a Batos Doxology of Palm Sunday, that is ⲇⲁⲩⲓⲇ ⲅⲁⲣ ⲡⲓϩⲩⲙⲛⲟⲧⲟⲥ...,[49] and also if they chose to a Batos Doxology of Palm Sunday, that is Ⲫⲏⲉⲧϩⲉⲙⲥⲓ ϩⲓϫⲉⲛ ⲛⲓⲭⲉⲣⲟⲩⲃⲓⲙ.[50] Then they say, Ⲧⲉⲛϭⲓⲥⲓ ⲘⲘⲞ...[51] and the Symbol of Faith[52]. They raise the cross[53] and pray Kyrie eleison in the Great Tune. Then they pray the Litany of the Gospel, read the Psalm and the Gospel in the Annual Tune, and respond saying Ⲭⲉⲣⲉ Ⲗⲁⲍⲁⲣⲟⲥ...[54] The prayer is then continued as usual until the Absolution of the Son.

---

[46] The expression "They raise incense as usual" means that the Litany of the Departed is prayed after the thanksgiving prayer. I have explained this in detail in the book "The Prayers of Raising of Incense of Vespers and Matins" and another time in the book "The Virginial Birth and the Divine Manifestation." It is also sufficient here to point out that *The Guide and Order of the Passion Week and the Glorious Passover Feast* (1920) mentions in p. 23: "They raise incense as usual and then say Ⲛⲓⲯⲩⲭⲏ and read the Doxologies..."

[47] That is: "Graciously accord, O Lord, to keep up this day..."

[48] The manuscript includes the full text of this Doxology in Coptic only.

[49] The same as the previous footnote.

[50] The same as the previous footnote.

[51] That is, "We exalt you, the mother of the true Light..."

[52] That is the Creed.

[53] While the Church Order Manuscripts only mention the expression "they raise the cross," which is a very old liturgical practice which I explain in other books, *The Guide and Order of the Passion Week and the Glorious Passover Feast* (1920) adds: "the priest says Ⲫϯ ⲚⲀⲒ ⲚⲀⲚ (Evnoti Nay Nan) and the congregation prays Kyrie eleison in the Great Tune."

[54] That is (Shere Lazarus): "Hail to Lazarus..." The manuscript only includes these words as the beginning of the response.

Afterwards, they light up candles and chant the Hosanna Hymn of Ⲉⲩⲗⲟⲅⲏⲙⲉⲛⲟⲥ... while still in the chorus. When they reach the first Hosanna, they proceed to the icon of Palm Sunday if available and continue the rest of the hymn. The Hosanna is prayed in the Short Tune of the Cross, followed by the reading of the Commentary along with its translation. Afterwards, they say ˙Ⲡⲟⲩⲣⲟ ˋⲛⲧⲉ ϯϩⲓⲣⲏⲛⲏ...[55] until the end, raise the Bible and the cross and pray Kyrie eleison. As the congregation kisses them, the deacons chant this canon[56] with the Hosanna Tune, the Tune of Paul of Vespers and Matins: Ⲣⲁϣⲓ ⲟⲩⲛⲟϥ Ⲥⲓⲱⲛ ϯⲃⲁⲕⲓ...[57,58]

2. Commentary on some Liturgical Aspects of the Vespers of Palm Sunday

The Doxologies of Palm Sunday

In addition to the aforementioned Batos Doxology included in the *Manuscript of the Roman Quarter Typikon (15ᵗʰ century)*, there are three other doxologies that appeared in the published Psalmodies.

---

[55] That is: "O King of peace..."
[56] Here, the Commentary is read for the second time, the first being in the Vespers Praise of the Feast.
[57] The manuscript includes the full text of the canon in Coptic. I will include it along with its translation later.
[58] The same is mentioned by the *Church Order Manuscript No. 73 (Rite) in Cairo Patriarchate for the year 1444* and the other Church Order manuscripts.

The First Doxology

It begins in the same manner as the Psali of Palm Sunday, "Blow at the New Moon with the sound of the trumpet...," and it is made up of ten verses. Although it includes similar meanings to the Psali, the latter retains a more exuberant tone.

The Doxology wonders in amazement at the Lord's entry into Jerusalem on a colt while He sits upon the Cherubim, saying: "Oh what great humility?" Then it continues with the following verses, which are not mentioned in the Psali:

- Offer to the Lord, O sons of God, offer to the Lord glory and honour. Rejoice in our God, with doxologies of blessing.
- Praise is due to You O God in Zion and Jerusalem. They send to You prayers unto the ages.
- We praise and glorify Him, and exalt Him above all, as a Good One and Lover of Man, have mercy upon us according to Your great mercy.

The Second Doxology

It is comprised of eight verses, and does not include many new meanings, save for saying:

> You have perfected praise according to Your will, O Lord.

The Third Doxology

It is comprised of ten verses and proclaims that the praises and shouts of the children was divinely inspired, for they did not utter these simply of their own accord, but to fulfil the Lord's will. This same notion was briefly noted in the second doxology in the aforementioned verse.

Some of its verses are as follows:
- The Gospels have witnessed, saying likewise: He rode on a donkey as a symbol of the Cherubim.
- And the teachers of the Church cried out saying: Blessed is the Lord Jesus, who came and saved us.
- We also praise Him with the blessed children who were taught by the Holy Spirit: "Hosanna to the Son of David."
- Blessed is He who comes in the name of the Lord of hosts, and in His Second Coming He is exalted above all forever.

After the Doxologies of Palm Sunday, they pray what is appropriate from the other doxologies. In a lordly feast, aside from the holy Paschal Week, the doxologies of St. Mary, the martyrs, and the saints may be chanted if time permits.[59]

The Vespers Gospel Reading of Palm Sunday

---

[59] Some of the new liturgical references, like *The Guide and Order of the Passion Week and the Glorious Passover Feast* (1920), mention that the Hosanna Praises, which are new, are to be chanted after the Doxologies.

The Gospel Reading (John 12) is about the communal meal Martha, Mary and Lazarus held for Jesus in Bethany six days before Passover, and Lazarus was one of those at table with Him. A great crowd of the Jews came, not only on account of Jesus, but also to see Lazarus who was raised from the dead. In this banquet, Mary, Lazarus' sister, poured costly ointment of pure nard[60] on the Lord's feet such that the house was filled with its fragrance.

This Gospel Reading was not mentioned by Ibn Kabar (1324 AD), but it is the same one found in the Lectionary of the Church of Jerusalem which is read on Lazarus Saturday. It is also the same Gospel Reading that the Byzantine Church reads on Holy Paschal Monday.[61]

The Vespers Gospel Response of Palm Sunday
After the Gospel Reading, they respond saying:

---

[60] The nard ointment is extracted from the spikenard tree – a small sized tree that grows on high mountain tops. The Indians have used it in the old days as a remedy of certain illnesses. It is very costly. Refer to: Song of Songs 1:12, 4:13-14.
[61] Dom Emmaneul Lanne, *op. cit.*, 286.

Hail to Lazarus whom You raised,[62] after four days. Raise my heart O my Lord Jesus, that was killed by the evil one.

It is the same Gospel Response that was recited in the morning of the same day. In the morning, the Gospel Reading was about Lazarus whom the Lord raised from the dead. In the evening, in the Eve of Palm Sunday, the Gospel also revolves around the gathering in Lazarus' house. Let us leave Mary's ointment and the spikenard and proceed to another account.

The Liturgically Correct Place of the Hosanna Hymn

The Church Order manuscripts, as well as the other manuscripts under study, specify that the liturgical elements of the Palm Sunday Vespers Raising of Incense Prayer are the Doxologies and the Gospel Response. As mentioned before, they reserve the Hosanna Hymn until at the end of the prayer after the Absolution of the Son and before the Conclusion Prayer.

On the other hand, *The Typikon and Order of the Passion Week and the Glorious Passover Feast for the year (1920)* places the Hosanna Hymn after the

---

[62] "You raised" according to the Church Order manuscripts, and not "He raised" in the third person form.

priest says Ⲫϯ ⲚⲀⲒ ⲚⲀⲚ (Evnoti Nay Nan), that is "O God, have mercy upon us," and the congregation prays Kyrie eleison in the Great Tune. The Commentary, which was omitted from the Feast's Vespers Praise, is then read after the Hymn. In its second edition for the year 1987, the Typikon includes a Coptic and Arabic response after the Hosanna Hymn, which reads ⲰⲤⲀⲚⲚⲀ ⲎⲈⲚ ⲚⲎⲈⲦϬⲞⲤⲒ, "Hosanna in the highest..." This response was omitted in the first edition of 1920 despite being an authentic and original response to the Hosanna Hymn and is mentioned in the Church Order manuscripts, which state:

> ... they continue the rest of the Hymn and then say Hosanna in the Tune of the Cross.

I cannot say that the difference between the rite mentioned in the Typikon of 1920 and what came in the Church Order manuscripts is a distinct practice known in only some regions. In fact, it was an intentional modification in the rite by those who wrote the Typikon for the evident reason mentioned in the Typikon itself in p. 31, saying:

> They continue the prayer as usual. If an icon of Palm Sunday is available, they light up candles and proceed towards it, chanting the Hosanna Hymn

of Ⲉⲩⲗⲟⲅⲏⲙⲉⲛⲟⲥ. Then the Commentary is read, followed by this canon...

Therefore, it is unreasonable to chant the Hosanna Hymn and its Commentary before reading the Gospel, then repeat them after the Gospel Reading and the Absolution of the Son, that is less than ten minutes later.

If we chant the Hosanna Hymn before the Vespers Gospel Reading, in accordance with what came in the 1920 Typikon, then why should we ignore what appeared in the same Typikon concerning chanting the Hymn and the Commentary at the end of the Vespers Prayers before the Concluding Prayer? Thus, we have two possibilities: either to return to the original rite before 1920 in accordance with the Church Order manuscripts, or for the Church to publish a Typikon that legitimises the rite and order of Vespers of Palm Sunday.

The Concluding Prayers of the Vespers and Matins of Palm Sunday

The canon of the Concluding Prayers is one of the most neglected liturgical elements in our churches these days. These canons are supposed to be a concluding prayer that summarises the events of the occasion celebrated by the Church, but the vast majority of these have been abbreviated to one or two brief phrases.

The current canon of the Concluding Prayers in the Vespers and Matins of Palm Sunday is actually a very old one that is found in the oldest Psalmody Manuscripts known today. It is kept, for example, in *Manuscript No. 3 (Coptic) in the Library of Vienna (Austria)*, which goes back to the fifteenth century or possibly even earlier.[63]

It is also kept in *Manuscript No. 221 (Rite) in the Library of Macarius Monastery*, which goes back to the fourteenth century and is one of the oldest Coptic Psalmody Manuscripts known in the world to date.[64]

I include the full text of the canon as it appeared in the manuscripts and will footnote the slight differences that appeared in the Typikon.

---

[63] The Manuscript of Vienna includes a large number of canons of Concluding Prayers in Coptic only. It includes eight canons for the Lordly Feasts of Annunciation, Nativity, Epiphany, Palm Sunday, Resurrection (2 canons), Ascension, and Pentecost. Therefore, the canon of Palm Sunday is numbered (4).
[64] I have made an inventory of the Annual and Koiak Psalmody Manuscripts in the libraries of Egypt and around the world, which I include at the end of the second edition of the book "The Praises of Midnight and Lauds."

The reader may notice how the canon focuses in each verse on the praises and cries of the children, saying: "Hosanna in the highest, this is the King of Israel."

This repeated recitation of a biblical verse is a unique Coptic characteristic, recited by all the congregation during the liturgical prayers in Church, especially on Lordly Feasts, and mainly featured in the canon of Concluding Prayers or in the Psalis or Commentaries. This feature can also be found in other Lordly Feasts, for example in the Feasts of Nativity and Resurrection.

(4) Canon of Palm Sunday	=ⲇ̅. ⲕⲁⲛⲱⲛ ⲡⲓⲉⲩⲗⲟⲅⲓⲙⲉⲛⲟⲥ[65]
Rejoice and be glad O city of Zion. Reign[66] and be glad for behold your King shall come riding on a colt.	Ⲣⲁϣⲓ ⲟⲩⲛⲟϥ Ⲥⲓⲱⲛ ϯⲃⲁⲕⲓ : ⲟⲓ ⲉⲣⲟⲩⲣⲟ ⲟⲩⲟϩ ⲑⲉⲗⲏⲗ : ϩⲏⲡⲡⲉ ⲅⲁⲣ ⲡⲉⲟⲩⲣⲟ `ϥⲛⲏⲟⲩ : ⲉϥⲧⲁⲗⲏⲟⲩⲧ ` ⲉϫⲉⲛ ⲟⲩⲥⲏϫ .
Before Him the children praise saying, "Hosanna in the highest, this is the King of Israel."	Ⲉⲩϩⲱⲥ ϧ'ⲁϫⲱϥ `ⲛϫⲉ ⲛⲓⲁⲗⲱⲟⲩ`ⲓ : ϫⲉ `ⲱⲥⲁⲛⲛⲁ ϧ'ⲉⲛ ⲛⲏⲉⲧϭⲟⲥⲓ : ⲫⲁⲓ ⲡⲉ ` ⲡⲟⲩⲣⲟ `ⲙⲠⲓⲥⲣⲁⲏⲗ .
Glory be...	ⲇⲟ̅ⲝ̅ⲁ̅ ...

---

[65] The text of this canon can be found in the manuscript in pages 168 (front) till 169 (front).
[66] In the Guide: "Rejoice" ϭⲓⲉⲣⲟⲩⲟⲧ

Book I: Lazarus Saturday and Palm Sunday

When Christ[67] came to the city of Jerusalem to fulfil the scriptures of the chosen prophets,	Ⲉⲧⲁϥ`ⲓ `ⲛϫⲉ Ⲡ̅ⲭ̅ⲥ̅ : `ⲉϯⲃⲁⲕⲓ Ⲓⲉⲣⲟⲩⲥⲁⲗⲏⲙ : `ⲉϫⲱⲕ `ⲉⲃⲟⲗ `ⲛⲛⲓⲅⲣⲁⲫⲏ : `ⲛⲧⲉ ⲛⲓⲥⲱⲧⲡ `ⲙ` ⲡⲣⲟⲫⲏⲧⲏⲥ .
the children carried palm branches saying, "Hosanna in the highest, this is the King of Israel."	ⲁ ⲛⲓ `ⲁⲗⲱⲟⲩ`ⲓ ϥⲁⲓ `ⲛ̅ⲍⲁⲛⲃⲁⲓ : ϫⲉ `ⲱⲥⲁⲛⲛⲁ `ϧⲉⲛ ⲛⲏⲉⲧϭⲟⲥⲓ : ⲫⲁⲓ ⲡⲉ `ⲡⲟⲩⲣⲟ `ⲙ̅Ⲡⲓⲥⲣⲁⲏⲗ .
Now...	=Ⲛ̅ⲩ̅ⲛ̅ ...
Some spread their garments on the road before Him that Jesus the Nazarene may walk on them, and the infants proclaim and say, "Hosanna in the highest, this is the King of Israel."	ⲁ ϩⲁⲛⲟⲩⲟⲛ ⲫⲱⲣϣ `ⲛ̅ⲛⲟⲩ `ϩⲃⲱⲥ : ϩⲓϫⲉⲛ ⲡⲓⲙⲱⲓⲧ `ⲙⲡⲉϥ `ⲙⲑⲟ : ϩⲓⲛⲁ ` ⲛⲧⲉϥⲙⲟϣⲓ `ⲉ `ϩⲣⲏⲓ `ⲉϫⲱⲟⲩ : `ⲛϫⲉ Ⲓⲏⲥⲟⲩⲥ ⲡⲓⲛⲁⲍⲱⲣⲉⲟⲥ : `ⲉⲣⲉ ⲛⲓⲕⲟⲩϫⲓ ⲱϣ `ⲉⲃⲟⲗ : ϫⲉ `ⲱⲥⲁⲛⲛⲁ ϧⲉⲛ ⲛⲏⲉⲧϭⲟⲥⲓ : ⲫⲁⲓ ⲡⲉ `ⲡⲟⲩⲣⲟ ` ⲙ̅Ⲡⲓⲥⲣⲁⲏⲗ .
Now...	Ⲛ̅ⲩ̅ⲛ̅ ...
Then was fulfilled the great prophecy today, "Out of the mouths of children[68], You have prepared praise," and the children proclaim and say, "Hosanna in the highest, this is the King of Israel."	Ⲧⲟⲧⲉ ⲁⲥϫⲱⲕ `ⲉⲃⲟⲗ `ⲙ̅ⲫⲟⲟⲩ : ` ⲛϫⲉ ϯⲛⲓϣϯ `ⲙ `ⲡⲣⲟⲫⲏⲧⲓⲁ : ` ⲉⲃⲟⲗϧⲉⲛ ⲣⲱⲟⲩ `ⲛ̅ϩⲁⲛ `ⲁⲗⲱⲟⲩ `ⲓ : ` ⲛⲑⲟⲕ ⲁⲕⲥⲉⲃⲧⲉ ⲡⲓ `ⲥⲙⲟⲩ : `ⲉⲣⲉ ⲛⲓ ` ⲁⲗⲱⲟⲩ `ⲓ ⲱϣ `ⲉⲃⲟⲗ : ϫⲉ `ⲱⲥⲁⲛⲛⲁ ϧⲉⲛ ⲛⲏⲉⲧϭⲟⲥⲓ : ⲫⲁⲓ ⲡⲉ `ⲡⲟⲩⲣⲟ ` ⲙ̅Ⲡⲓⲥⲣⲁⲏⲗ .
Now...	Ⲛ̅ⲩ̅ⲛ̅ ...

---

[67] In the Guide: "our Lord Jesus Christ" Ⲡⲉⲛⲟ̅ⲥ̅ Ⲓ̅ⲏ̅ⲥ̅ Ⲡ̅ⲭ̅ⲥ̅
[68] In the Guide: "young children" in the entire canon.

Therefore, David said in the book of the Psalms, "Blessed is He who comes in the name of the Lord of hosts[69]," and the children proclaim and say, "Hosanna in the highest, this is the King of Israel." Now…	Ⲧⲟⲧⲉ ⲁϥϫⲟⲥ ⲛ̀ϫⲉ Ⲇⲁⲩⲓⲇ : ϧⲉⲛ ⲡϫⲱⲙ ⲛ̀ⲧⲉ ⲛⲓⲯⲁⲗⲙⲟⲥ : ϫⲉ ϥ̀ⲥⲙⲁⲣⲱⲟⲩⲧ ⲛ̀ϫⲉ ⲫⲏⲉⲑⲛⲏⲟⲩ : ϧⲉⲛ ⲫⲣⲁⲛ ⲙ̀Ⲡ𝛐̅ⲥ̅ ⲛ̀ⲧⲉ ⲛⲓϫⲟⲙ : ⲉⲣⲉ ⲛⲓⲕⲟⲩϫⲓ ⲱϣ ⲉⲃⲟⲗ : ϫⲉ ⲱ̀ⲥⲁⲛⲛⲁ ϧⲉⲛ ⲛⲏⲉⲧϭⲟⲥⲓ : ⲫⲁⲓ ⲡⲉ ⲡ̀ⲟⲩⲣⲟ ⲙ̀Ⲡⲓⲥⲣⲁⲏⲗ. =Ⲛ̅ⲩ̅ⲛ̅…
When Jesus entered Jerusalem, the whole city trembled because of the multitudes surrounding Him, and the children proclaim and say, "Hosanna in the highest, this is the King of Israel." Now…	Ⲉⲧⲁϥⲓ̀ ⲛ̀ϫⲉ Ⲓⲏⲥⲟⲩⲥ : ⲉ̀ϧⲟⲩⲛ ⲉ̀Ⲓⲉⲣⲟⲩⲥⲁⲗⲏⲙ : ⲁ ϯⲃⲁⲕⲓ ⲧⲏⲣⲥ ϣⲑⲟⲣⲧⲉⲣ : ⲉⲑⲃⲉ ⲛⲓⲙⲏϣ ⲉⲧⲕⲱϯ ⲉⲣⲟϥ : ⲉⲣⲉ ⲛⲓⲁ̀ⲗⲱⲟⲩⲓ̀ ⲱϣ ⲉⲃⲟⲗ : ϫⲉ ⲱ̀ⲥⲁⲛⲛⲁ ϧⲉⲛ ⲛⲏⲉⲧϭⲟⲥⲓ : ⲫⲁⲓ ⲡⲉ ⲡ̀ⲟⲩⲣⲟ ⲙ̀Ⲡⲓⲥⲣⲁⲏⲗ. =Ⲛ̅ⲩ̅ⲛ̅…
Then, the lawless Jews were filled with great jealousy and said to our Lord[70] Jesus, "Let the infants stop saying, 'Hosanna in the highest, this is the King of Israel.'" Now…	Ⲧⲟⲧⲉ ⲛⲓⲒⲟⲩⲇⲁⲓ ⲛ̀ⲁⲛⲟⲙⲟⲥ : ⲁⲩⲙⲟϩ ⲉⲃⲟⲗϧⲉⲛ ⲟⲩⲛⲓϣϯ ⲛ̀ⲭⲟϩ : ⲡⲉϫⲱⲟⲩ ⲙ̀ⲡⲉⲛ𝛐̅ⲥ̅ Ⲓⲏⲥⲟⲩⲥ : ϫⲉ ⲙⲁⲣⲟⲩⲭⲁⲣⲱⲟⲩ ⲛ̀ϫⲉ ⲛⲓⲕⲟⲩϫⲓ ⲛ̀ ⲁⲗⲱⲟⲩⲓ̀ : ϫⲉ ⲱ̀ⲥⲁⲛⲛⲁ ϧⲉⲛ ⲛⲏⲉⲧϭⲟⲥⲓ : ⲫⲁⲓ ⲡⲉ ⲡ̀ⲟⲩⲣⲟ ⲙ̀Ⲡⲓⲥⲣⲁⲏⲗ. =Ⲛ̅ⲩ̅ⲛ̅…
Then Jesus said to the Jews, "If the infants	Ⲡⲉϫⲉ Ⲓⲏⲥⲟⲩⲥ ⲛ̀ⲛⲓⲒⲟⲩⲇⲁⲓ : ϫⲉ ⲉϣⲱⲡ ⲁⲩϣⲁⲛⲭⲁⲣⲱⲟⲩ : ⲛ̀ϫⲉ ϩⲁⲛ-

---

[69] In the Guide: "the Lord God" ⲙ̀Ⲡ𝛐̅ⲥ̅ Ⲫϯ
[70] In the Guide: "to the Lord."

should keep silent, the stones would cry out and praise Me saying, 'Hosanna in the highest, this is the King of Israel.'"	ⲕⲟⲩϫⲓ ⳿ⲛ⳿ⲁⲗⲱⲟⲩ⳿ⲓ : ϣⲁⲩⲱϣ ⳿ⲉⲃⲟⲗ ⳿ⲛϫⲉ ⲛⲓ⳿ⲱⲛⲓ : ⲟⲩⲟϩ ⳿ⲛⲧⲟⲩϩⲱⲥ ⳿ ⲉⲣⲟⲓ : ϫⲉ ⳿ⲱⲥⲁⲛⲛⲁ ϧⲉⲛ ⲛⲏⲉⲧϭⲟⲥⲓ : ⲫⲁⲓ ⲡⲉ ⳿ⲡⲟⲩⲣⲟ ⳿ⲙⲠⲓⲥⲣⲁⲏⲗ .
We proclaim saying…	Ⲉⲛⲱϣ …

At the end, the priest concludes the prayer with the blessing as usual and dismisses the congregation in peace that they may rest for a while at home.

Chapter Three: The Rite of Praises of Midnight and Lauds on Palm Sunday

First: According to the Manuscripts and the Old Liturgical References

According to Ibn Kabar,

In the Manuscript of Paris:

> ... the Psalmody is prayed in full.

In the Manuscript of Uppsala:

> ... they complete the Midnight Prayer and the Psalmody and say the Canticle that starts with ⲁⲓⲟⲩⲛⲟϥ `ⲉϫⲉⲛ ⲛⲏ.[1]

In the Other Manuscripts Under Study

The *Manuscript of the Roman Quarter Typikon (15th century)* attributes to the Great Canticle the title "The Canticle chanted with the Annual Tune after the Midnight Psalms." This Canticle is the only liturgical element mentioned by this manuscript in the Praises of Midnight and Lauds for Palm Sunday.

---

[1] The *Manuscript of the Patriarchate* completes the missing phrase in the *Manuscript of Uppsala*, saying: ⲁⲓⲟⲩⲛⲟϥ `ⲉϫⲉⲛ ⲛⲏ `ⲉⲧⲁⲩϫⲟⲥ ⲛⲏⲓ, that is "I was glad when they said to me..."

The *Manuscript of London Typikon* states the following after pointing out what is to be read in the Vespers Raising of Incense on Palm Sunday:

> ... the prayer is concluded with the benediction. They rest for a while and then start the Midnight Prayer as usual. After reading the Psalms, they say Kyrie eleison and the Canticle that appropriate for the feast, followed by the four canticles as usual and the Psali of the feast. They then read the Theotokion and conclude the prayer as usual.

In the Church Order Manuscripts

The *Church Order Manuscript No. 118 (Rites) in Cairo Patriarchate 1911* mentions the following under the title "The Midnight Prayer of Palm Sunday":[2]

> They begin[3] the Annual Midnight Prayer as usual. After reciting the Psalms, they chant Alleluia in the Annual Tune[4]. Then they read the Canticle of the feast in Coptic, which is Oγωn̄ 'eβολ 'м̄Пос ϧen oγкγθapa...[5] until the end. When the reader finishes, the Canticle is then interpreted in Arabic as follows: From the praises of David the prophet, may his blessings be with us, Amen. Praise the Lord with the harp...[6]. After the interpretation, the reader

---

[2] The same is mentioned by the *Manuscript of Al-Baramūs Monastery for the year 1514*.
[3] The word is misspelled in the manuscript.
[4] This Tune is known for "Midnight Alleluia."
[5] That is "Praise the Lord with the harp..." The manuscript includes the full text of the Canticle of Palm Sunday in Coptic.
[6] The manuscript includes the full text of the Canticle of Palm Sunday in Arabic.

says `ⲤⲘⲞⲨ ʼⲈⲢⲞⲒ ... Γ̄`[7] as usual and they respond[8] with Doxa Patri three times[9], followed by Ⲕⲉ ⲚⲨⲚ.[10] Then, they say[11] Alleluia Kyrie eleison as usual. The four canticles are then prayed as usual. After ` ⲤⲘⲞⲨ ʼⲈⲠⲞⲤ, they read[12] the Psalis of the feast and Ⲥⲉⲙⲟⲩϯ until the end and continue[13] the Midnight Prayer as is customary.

Second: Commentary on the Midnight Praise of Palm Sunday

They start the Midnight Prayer as usual. After the Midnight Alleluia, they say the Canticle of Palm Sunday, which is also called the "Great Canticle."

The Great Canticle in the Midnight Praise of Palm Sunday

Ibn Kabar – in accordance with the *Manuscript of Uppsala of 1546* – includes the first two words of the Great Canticle of Palm Sunday, which reveals that it is different from the Great Canticle mentioned in the *Manuscript of Al-Baramūs Monastery for the year 1514* and in the *Church Order Manuscript No. 118 (Rites) in Cairo Patriarchate for the year 1911*, as well as in the other manuscripts under study.

---

[7] That is: Bless me (three times).
[8] The word is misspelled in the manuscript.
[9] That is: Glory to the Father and the Son and the Holy Spirit (three times).
[10] That is: Now and ever and unto the age of ages. Amen.
[11] The word is misspelled in the manuscript.
[12] The word is misspelled in the manuscript.
[13] The word is misspelled in the manuscript.

Thus, until the sixteenth century, there were at least two Great Canticles in the Midnight Praise of Palm Sunday, but only one survived and the other did not.

The Church Order manuscript include this Canticle composed of 24 verses, while *The Typikon and Order of the Passion Week and the Glorious Passover Feast (1920)* includes the same Canticle but divided into 30 verses in addition to another two verses, one in the beginning[14] and the other in the middle.[15]

The following is the full text of this Canticle according to the translation and the verse division of the *Church*

---

[14] Which is: O, sing to the Lord a new song. Sing to the Lord all the earth. Sing to the Lord and bless His name. Proclaim the good news of His salvation from day to day. Declare His glory among the nations, and His wonders among all peoples. For the Lord is great and greatly to be blessed. He is to be feared above all gods. Alleluia.
This verse is also included in the manuscripts under study. However, there is no consensus among the manuscripts regarding the number of verses of the Great Canticle.
[15] Which is: This is the day the Lord has made. We will rejoice and be glad in it. Save, O Lord. O Lord, ease our ways. Blessed is He who comes in the name of the Lord. Bind the sacrifice with cords to the horns of the altar. Alleluia.
This verse is also included in the *Manuscript of the Roman Quarter Typikon (15th century)*, but not in the *Manuscript of Abba Shenoute Typikon (14th century)* or the manuscripts of the Hanging Church Typikon.

Order Manuscript No. 118 (Rites) in Cairo Patriarchate for the year 1911[16].

1) Praise the Lord with the harp. Make melody to Him with an instrument of ten strings. Sing to Him a new song. Sing with a shout of joy. For the word of the Lord is right, and all His work is done in truth. He loves mercy and justice. The earth is full of the mercy of the Lord. Alleluia.
2) Sing to God. Sing praises to His name. Extol Him who rides on the clouds. The Lord is His name.
3) Rejoice before Him. Tremble before His face. For He is a father of the fatherless, a defender of widows. Alleluia.
4) O Lord, our Lord, how excellent is Your name in all the earth. You have set Your glory above the heavens. Out of the mouth of babes and nursing infants[17] You have prepared praise. Alleluia.
5) Sing praises to the Lord, who dwells in Zion. Declare His deeds among the people. When He avenges blood, He remembers them. He does not forget the cry of the humble. Alleluia.
6) In the midst of the assembly I will praise You. I will declare Your name to My brethren. You who fear the Lord, praise Him. All you descendants of Jacob, glorify Him, and fear Him all you offspring of Israel. Alleluia.
7) One thing I have desired of the Lord, and that will I seek: That I may dwell in the house of the Lord all the days of my life. Alleluia.
8) Let Mount Zion rejoice, and let the daughters of Judah be glad because of Your judgments, O Lord. Walk about Zion, and go all around her. Count her towers. Alleluia.

---

[16] The manuscript includes the Coptic text of this Canticle, followed by the Arabic interpretation.
[17] That is "suckling."

9) You are God. Praise is due to You in Zion, and to You the vow shall be performed in Jerusalem. Alleluia.
10) Blessed be the Lord, the God of Israel, Who only does wondrous things. Blessed be His glorious and holy name forever and ever. Alleluia.
11) Blow the trumpet at the time of the New Moon, on your solemn feast day, for this is a statute for Israel and a law of the God of Jacob. Alleluia.
12) O come, let us sing to the Lord. Let us shout joyfully to God, our salvation. Let us come before His presence with thanksgiving. Let us shout joyfully to Him with psalms, for the Lord is the great God[18]. Alleluia.
13) Praise the Lord, O children. Bless the name of the Lord. Let the name of the Lord be blessed now and forevermore. From the rising of the sun to its going down bless the name of the Lord. Alleluia.
14) O house of Israel, trust in the Lord. He is their help and their shield. O house of Levi, trust in the Lord. He is their help and their shield. You who fear the Lord, trust in the Lord. He is their help and their shield.[19] Alleluia.
15) I was glad when they said to me, "Let us go into the house of the Lord." Our feet have been standing within your gates, O Jerusalem.[20] Jerusalem is built as a city that is compact together, where the tribes go up, the tribes of the Lord, as a testimony for Israel, to give thanks to the name of the Lord. Alleluia.
16) Those who trust in the Lord are like Mount Zion, which cannot be moved. As the mountains surround Jerusalem,

---

[18] ⲘⲀⲢⲈⲚ`ⲰⲖⲎⲖⲞⲨ`Ⲓ ⲚⲀϤ ϦⲈⲚ ϨⲀⲚⲮⲀⲖⲘⲞⲤ. ϪⲈ `ⲚⲐⲞϤ ⲞⲨⲚⲒⲰϮ `ⲚⲚⲞⲨϮ Ⲡ̅ⲟ̅ⲥ̅. ⲁ̅ⲗ̅

[19] Then comes the verse of "This is the day the Lord has made. We will rejoice and be glad in it…"

[20] According to the manuscript: "Our feet have been standing within the gates of Jerusalem"

so the Lord surrounds His people from now and forever.[21] Alleluia.

17) Praise the Lord for He is good.[22] Praise the Lord, O you servants of the Lord, you who stand in the house of the Lord, in the courts[23] of the house of our God. Alleluia.

18) Bless the Lord, O house of Aaron. Bless the Lord, O house of Levi. You who fear the Lord, bless the Lord. Blessed be the Lord out of Zion, Who dwells in Jerusalem. Alleluia.

19) Praise the Lord with a good psalm.[24] It is pleasant to sing praises to our God. The Lord builds up Jerusalem. He gathers together the outcasts of Israel.[25] Alleluia.

20) Praise the Lord, O Jerusalem. Glorify your God, O Zion. For He has strengthened the bars of your gates. He has blessed your children within you. He makes peace in your borders, and fills you with the finest wheat. Alleluia.

21) Let them exalt Him in the church of His people, and praise Him in the seat of the elders, for He has made the family like a flock of sheep. The upright shall see and rejoice. Alleluia.

22) The Lord has sworn and will have no regret, "You are a priest forever after the order of Melchizedek." Alleluia.

23) God be merciful to us and bless us, and cause His face to shine upon us. O Lord, save Your people and bless Your inheritance. Shepherd them all, and bear them up forever. Alleluia.

24) Whoever is wise...

---

[21] The manuscript includes the following Coptic text: ⲓⲥϫⲉⲛ ϯⲛⲟⲩ ⲛⲉⲙ ϣⲁ ⲉⲛⲉϩ, that is "from now and forever." However, this is not included in the Guide of 1920.

[22] ⲤⲘⲞⲨ ⲉⲠϭⲞⲤ ϫⲉ ⲞⲨⲀⲄⲀⲐⲞⲤ ⲠⲈ Ⲡϭⲟⲥ.

[23] According to the manuscript: "in the home."

[24] According to the manuscript: "with a good saying."

[25] ⲚⲒϪⲰⲢ ⲈⲂⲞⲖ ⲚⲦⲈ ⲠⲒⲤⲖ Ⲡϭⲥ ⲚⲀⲐⲞⲨⲰⲦⲞⲨ.

The *Church Order Manuscript No. 118 (Rites) in Cairo Patriarchate for the year 1911* includes at the end of the Great Canticle a remarkable rite, which was not mentioned in *The Typikon and Order of the Passion Week and the Glorious Passover Feast (1920)*, as it indicates that after the reader has finished the Great Canticle, he would say "Bless me" three times as usual, and they respond to him three times saying "Glory to the Father and the Son and the Holy Spirit," and then continue saying "Now and ever and unto the age of ages. Amen."[26]

After the Great Canticle, they begin praying the four canticles as usual, and at the end the Psalis of the feast, followed by the Sunday Theotokia. Afterwards, the Midnight Praise is continued as is customary.

The Canticle Psalis in the Midnight Praise of Palm Sunday

As previously noted, the manuscripts under study seem to have the same order for the Midnight Praise of Palm Sunday as do the Church Order manuscripts.

It is evident from *The Typikon and Order of the Passion Week and the Glorious Passover Feast (1920)* that until 1911 there was no mention of Psalis for the Canticles or the

---

[26] Why did we discontinue such beautiful liturgical practices from our marvellous Coptic Rite?

Commemoration, while this Typikon includes five Adam Psalis for the four Canticles and the Theotokia, and a sixth Batos Psali for the Commemoration. As mentioned before, the manuscripts include only two Psalis for the feast, the first is Batos which, according to the published Typikon, is said on the Commemoration, and the other is Adam, which is said on the first Canticle.

Thus, it seems that *The Typikon and Order of the Passion Week and the Glorious Passover Feast (1920)* found several Psalis for Palm Sunday, which it distributed on the liturgical elements of the Midnight Praise, that is the Canticles, the Commemoration and the Theotokia. However, this innovation is neither supported by the old liturgical references nor the manuscripts under study.

The style of these Psalis follows that of Nicodemus,[27] who also composed many Psalis for other ecclesiastical feasts and occasions. However, he is a rather inept composer, whose Psalis lack depth as well as commitment to the occasion which he writes for often deviating to other topics. More importantly, he removed

---

[27] The *Manuscript of Abba Shenoute Typikon (14th century)* includes the Psali of Palm Sunday, whose style matches that of Nicodemus. This piece of information gives us a hint about the time period in which he lived. Research is needed for determining the exact period, however.

the Psali from its old initial context of a prayer addressing the Lord Jesus, which is the main feature that distinguishes Psalis from Doxologies.

The composer of these many Psalis mention his name in some of them, but not in others. However, there are two main features that distinguish his Psalis, which can be found in each one he wrote, regardless of whether he mentions his name.

The First Feature: He so longed to visit Jerusalem to see the Saviour's tomb – a strong desire that overshadowed other themes.

In the Palm Sunday Psali of the First Canticle,[28] he says:
- Blessed are You in truth, grant us to see the city of the Lord, the place of the tomb.
- And also the mountain of Kranion and the place of the crucifixion of our King, and the cave.
- The land of the Jordan, the place of the forgiveness of sins, and the baptism of John, grant us to see them.
- Guard us O Christ and grant us to see Bethlehem, O God, and the tomb of Your Mother.

In the Adam Psali of the Palm Sunday Theotokia, he says:
- The Mount of Kranion, the place where You were crucified, give us O King of glory to observe it.

---

[28] which is the only Psali that came in the manuscripts.

- Also the Resurrection of our Saviour the Christ and the land of the Jordan and the baptism of John.
- And the place of the tomb that is full of grace, in that place forgive us our trespasses.
- Hail to the Kranion, hail to the city of the Lord, hail to the tomb and the Resurrection.

The Second Feature: He prays for the souls of the departed in the verse before the last of his Psalis.

In the Adam Psali of Palm Sunday First Canticle, he says:
- The souls of our fathers repose them O Christ, because of Your Mother the Theotokos, the Virgin Mary.

In the Batos Psali of the Commemoration, he says:
- The souls of our fathers praise before God, proclaiming with the children and saying, "Hosanna in the highest."

In the Adam Psali of Palm Sunday Theotokia, he says:
- Repose the souls in Paradise, give us and them a share, O Christ.

The Palm Sunday Praise in the Syriac Church of Antioch

In the evening of Palm Sunday, the Syriac Church celebrates an order called "Order of the Lights," which is practiced when darkness falls after the first two watches of the Night Prayer. The clergy and the people gather in the church and begin the prayers of the rite, alternating between two choruses. The prayers focus on the importance of watchfulness and vigilance, as well as practicing faithfulness and good deeds in anticipation of the approach of the heavenly Bridegroom so as to enter with Him into the joys of the marriage feast.

The officiator of the prayer proclaims the start of the prayer following the Glorification saying,

> Grant us, O Christ our Lord, to light up the lamps of our souls with the oil of Your mercy, like the wise virgins, and to wait for You in watchfulness and vigilance, O heavenly Bridegroom, that we may enter with You into Your chamber full of joy, and give You glory and thanksgiving...

This is succeeded by several hymns and prayers the Gospel Reading, when the servants of the altar and clergy raise the cross and two candles and circumambulate towards the middle of the church nave. There, the leader of the prayer reads the Gospel of the ten virgins. The procession then continues outside the church through the northern door, and the congregation follows, each one holding a lit candle in their hand. The choir chants joyfully during this procession in the darkness of the night until everyone arrives at the main gate. Here are some of the verses:

> Glory be to the Good One who through His love revealed His glory to mankind... Let us all praise Him in glory before we fall asleep in death. In the long night, let us remember the death that silences and mutes our mouth. The righteous who kept watch through the nights remain

alive, even if they die, while the wicked who denied the glory of their Master are dead, even if they live. Let us arouse our souls in prayer and hymns in the Holy Spirit, and accompany the wise virgins whom our Lord praised, that we may behold the Bridegroom as we keep watch this night...

Then the officiator of the prayer kneels before the main gate and knocks on the door three times with the cross in his hand, while repeating these words "Your mercies, O Lord." After the third time, the door of the church is opened wide from the inside, and the church glistens radiantly with all its bright lights. The leader of the prayer and the clergy enter the church, followed by the congregation, as they continue the hymn the leader began when he knocked on the door saying, "Do not shut the door of Your mercies before us, O Lord. We confess that we are sinners. Have mercy on us." The ordo then concludes with a sermon that focuses on the purpose of this celebration, which is then followed by a hymn and the Concluding Prayer.

Interpretation of the Order: Walking in the dark with lit candles signifies the struggles and afflictions we undergo in our lives while guided by the light of faith. It is a continual journey that concludes with the arrival of the heavenly Bridegroom and our encounter with Him that we might participate in His eternal and joyful wedding feast. The church lit up with all its lights symbolises heaven with its eternal joy that awaits us.[29]

---

[29] *Our Liturgical Life*, 2nd year, No. 16 Azar (1991), 437.

Chapter Four: The Rites of Matins Raising of Incense Prayers of Palm Sunday

Introduction

In this chapter, I will divide the rite of the Matins Raising of Incense of Palm Sunday into three sections:

Section One: The rite of Matins Raising of Incense before the Hosanna Procession.

Section Two: The rite of the Hosanna Procession in the Matins Raising of Incense.

Section Three: The rite of what follows the Hosanna Procession until the end of the prayers of the Matins Raising of Incense.

Section One: The Rite of Matins Raising of Incense before the Hosanna Procession

First: Ibn Kabar
In the *Manuscript of Uppsala*:

> The Matins Prayer is offered as is customary on Sundays. They say the Theotokion, followed by Pan niben[1], and then

---

[1] It may be difficult for the reader to understand the liturgical location of the Theotokia in the Matins Raising of Incense from what is mentioned in the text of the *Manuscript of Uppsala* unless one has read the Order of Matins Raising of Incense in chapter 16

raise incense and say the Litanies of the Sick and the Oblations, the Praise of the Angels and what follows, the Creed and Kyrie eleison, followed by the Hymn of ⲈⲨⲖⲞⲄⲎⲘⲈⲚⲞⲤ...

Second: Ibn Sebā' in the Thirteenth Century

... in the evening of Lazarus Saturday, they cut palms and olive branches and weave them into one big honourable and glorious olive branch, adorned with crosses and candles, and carry it to the patriarch's cell. In the morning of that Sunday, that is Palm Sunday, the patriarch dons a green vestment, and they pray as is customary.[2] At the time of the Divine Liturgy, the patriarch wears the priestly garment as usual, while the priests and the deacons carry candles and Gospels. As the patriarch stands before the sanctuary, they carry the olive branch and chant before it the glorifications suitable to this feast. When they carry the olive branch, the patriarch proceeds to it at the central door, uncovers his head and places incense in the censer. The attending priests participate with him in the rites.

_____ Afterwards, he brings it to the sanctuary and places it by of this manuscript. I have explained this phenomenon in the second edition of the book "The Prayers of the Raising of Incense of Vespers and Matins."

I will summarise what appeared in both the *Manuscript of Paris* and the *Manuscript of Uppsala* about this section of the Matins Raising of Incense Prayer, in particular the location of the Psali and the Theotokia of the day. Both manuscripts agree on the following order of the Matins Raising of Incense:
- Adam Psali of Ⲡⲓⲟⲩⲱⲓⲛⲓ `ⲛⲧⲁ`ⲫⲙⲏⲓ "O True Light…"
- Adam Doxologies for the angles, the apostles, the martyrs, and the saints, which is said on all days of the week.

Only the *Manuscript of Uppsala* mentions that the Psali and the Theotokia of the day, whether Adam or Batos, are said here. Then, both manuscripts agree again on the following:

On the Adam days, they conclude with the Psali of Ⲛⲉⲕⲛⲁⲓ `ⲱ ⲡⲁⲛⲟⲩϯ "Your Mercies O my Lord."

On the Batos days, they say the Batos parts of the Batos Doxologies, which are:
- Seven archangels = Ⲍ̄`ⲛⲁⲣⲭⲏ ⲁⲅⲅⲉⲗⲟⲥ
- Our holy fathers the apostles Ⲛⲉⲛⲓⲟϯ ⲉ̄ⲑ̄ⲩ̄`ⲛⲁⲡⲟⲥⲧⲟⲗⲟⲥ
- The crowns of the martyrs Ⲛⲓ`ⲭⲗⲟⲙ `ⲛⲧⲉ ⲛⲓⲙ̄
- All the just who perfected Ⲛⲓ`ⲑⲙⲏⲓ ⲛⲓⲃⲉⲛ ⲉⲧⲁⲩϫⲱⲕ `ⲉⲃⲟⲗ
- Great is the honour Ⲟⲩⲛⲓϣϯ ⲅⲁⲣ ⲡⲉ ⲡⲓⲧⲁⲓⲟ

On the Batos days, they conclude with the Psali of "O our Lord Jesus Christ" `Ⲱ ⲡⲉⲛⲟ̄ⲥ̄ Ⲓ̄ⲏ̄ⲥ̄ Ⲡ̄ⲭ̄ⲥ̄.

Only the *Manuscript of Paris* mentions here that they raise incense and say the Praise of the Angels and a veneration for the Virgin "Hail to you, we ask you…" Ⲭⲉⲣⲉ ⲛⲉ ⲧⲉⲛϯϩⲟ ⲉⲣⲟ, followed by the Psali and the Theotokia of this day. However, if they were already recited in the Midnight Prayer, it is better not to repeat them again in the Matins. Some people would only repeat the final Lobsh (Explanation), the eight verses from the end, that is from letter Ⲱ to letter ϯ, and a few verses of Ⲛⲉⲕⲛⲁⲓ `ⲱ ⲡⲁⲛⲟⲩϯ.

Refer to: Wadi the Franciscan, *Christian Oriental Studies*, Volumes 35 and 36 (Cairo - Jerusalem: The Franciscan Centre of Christian Oriental Studies, 2003), 382-384, 403-405.

This is the location of the Psali and the Theotokia of the day according to the *Manuscript of Paris* in the fourteenth century and

the altar door.³

according to the *Manuscript of Uppsala* in the sixteenth century. Note that the liturgical placement of the Batos Doxologies lies before the start of the Matins Raising of Incense, which is mentioned in both manuscripts as I have previously pointed out. Two points are also important to note here:

First: When the *Manuscript of Uppsala* speaks of the Adam Psali "O True Light" it writes: "they say Tenoyωωτ before it" (Franciscan Brother Wadi', Volumes 35 and 36, *op. cit.*, p. 403). This is not mentioned in the *Manuscript of Paris*, which supports what I have repeatedly pointed out before that Tenoyωωτ is the older incipit of the Verses of Cymbals, which was not known in the Coptic Church before the fifteenth century.

Second: It came in the *Manuscript of Uppsala* that the one who arranged the Adam Psali of "O True Light" was "Pope Anba Benjamin in the churches of Egypt and before proliferating to the rest" (Wadi the Franciscan, Volumes 35 and 36, *op. cit.*, p. 403). This is probably Pope Benjamin the First (623-662 AD), the 38th Patriarch of the Coptic Church, as it could not be Pope Benjamin II (1327-1339 AD), the 82nd Patriarch of the Coptic Church, since this Adam Psali is mentioned in the *Manuscript of Paris*.

The Annual Psalmody states that the parts (the Adam Doxologies for the angels, apostles, martyrs, and saints) that follow this Adam Psali were arranged by the monks of St. Antony's Monastery at the Red Sea. It is possible that they were the ones who translated these Adam Doxologies to Coptic, and from there spread to all Coptic churches.

² The phrase "At the time of the Holy Liturgy, the patriarch puts on the priestly garment as usual" is parenthetical and does not mean that what comes after pertains to the time of the Liturgy. However, Ibn Sebā' mentions it here to emphasise that when the patriarch wears a green vestment when he enters the church in the morning of Palm Sunday and during the prayers of the Matins Raising of Incense, while during the Holy Liturgy he wears the usual priestly garment, which is different from the green vestment that he was wearing when he entered the church. The text can therefore be better understood if we strike out this phrase from the middle. What confirms this fact is that right after this paragraph, Ibn Sebā' continues to say: "At the time of the service of the Holy Liturgy, the Patriarch goes up to sanctify…"

Commentary on the Hosanna Procession by Ibn Sebā'
The previous piece by Ibn Sebā' explains the rite of the patriarch's entry into the church before the commencement of the Matins Raising of Incense Prayers. The priests and deacons go up to the patriarch's cell, holding candles and Gospels while carrying the olive branch, and the patriarch goes down with them in this Hosanna Procession while they chant the suitable glorifications of this feast. The procession continues to the sanctuary, where the patriarch stops by its door. At this point, Ibn Sebā' goes on to explain the rite of the olive branch before the start of the Matins Raising of Incense Prayers, as they circumambulate the altar while carrying the olive branch. But Ibn Sebā' does not specify whether they circumambulate the altar only, or if they circle the church nave as well and then return to the sanctuary. However, he clearly specifies that when they descend from the sanctuary, the patriarch follows them out, uncovers his head and places incense in the censer, aided by the attending priests. They, then, place the olive branch by the main sanctuary door.

Note that, according to Ibn Sebā', this Hosanna Procession takes place before the start of, and not during, the Matins Raising of Incense Prayers. This is

---

[3] Yoḥanna Ibn Zakaria Ibn Sebā', *op. cit.*, 318.

also confirmed by Ibn Kabar (1324 AD) in his book, *The Lamp that Lights in the Darkness In Clarifying the Service (Miṣbāḥ al-ẓulma wa 'īḍāḥ al-khidma)*, when he speaks of the Hosanna Procession in the Matins Prayer saying,

> some people practice this after the Psalmody Prayer and before the Matins Prayers, while others practice it after the offering of the Matins Prayer and the Raising of Incense and before the Gospel Reading.[4]

Also note that Ibn Sebā' did not make any reference to the Gospel Readings that are read during the Hosanna Procession.

Third: Church Order Manuscript No. 118 (Rites) in Cairo Patriarchate of 1911

The manuscript reads:[5]

> They commence[6] the Matins Prayer as usual. They recite the psalms and say ⲦⲈⲚⲞⲨⲰϢⲦ...[7] until the end of ⲚⲈⲔⲚⲀⲒ ` ⲱ ⲠⲀⲚⲞⲨϯ.[8] The priest raises incense and recites the Litanies

---

[4] Shams al-Ri'āsa Abū al-Barakāt Ibn Kabar, *The Lamp of Darkness and the Clarification of the Service (Miṣbāḥ al-ẓulma wa 'īḍāḥ al-khidma)*, Manuscript No. 203 (Arabic), National Library in Paris, Section 18.
[5] with some corrections in the spelling
[6] This word was misspelt in the manuscript.
[7] That is the Adam Matins Doxology.
[8] The dear reader may understand now why the Church Order manuscripts mention ⲚⲈⲔⲚⲀⲒ ` ⲱ ⲠⲀⲚⲞⲨϯ after the Adam Matins Doxology. According to Ibn Kabar in the *Manuscript of Uppsala*, the Psali and the Theotokia of the day, followed by the Conclusion of

of the Sick and the Oblations, followed by the Praise of the Angels. The priest circles around the church and raises incense while they chant[9] the Doxologies, followed by Tenϭici[10] and the Creed.

Fourth: Manuscript of the Roman Quarter Typikon (15th century) and the Other Manuscripts

The first liturgical element mentioned in the *Manuscript of the Roman Quarter Typikon (15th century)* regarding the Matins Raising of Incense of Palm Sunday is the Matins Gospel Response. It then skips straight to the hymn of the feast which is chanted after the Praxis.

The *Abba Shenoute Typikon (14th century)* mentions the following:

> The Matins Prayer as usual. The prayer of ⲀⲘⲰⲒⲚⲒ. Thanksgiving and Psalm 50. Ⲡⲓⲟⲩⲱⲓⲛⲓ and the Matins Psalms. Afterwards, they raise incense after adorning the Cross with olive and palm branches in the likeness of the Hebrew children who received our Saviour as He was riding on a colt and entering Jerusalem, and they wrap another cloth around it if available. Then, the Litanies of the Sick and the Oblations are prayed, followed by the Praise

---

the Theotokia, was prayed at this very time. But, when they settled for praying the Psali and the Theotokia only in the Morning Praise before the psalms of the Matins Prayer (which Ibn Kabar insisted on in the *Manuscript of Paris*), it became sufficient here to read the Conclusion of the Theotokia as a trace of this ancient rite.

[9] This word was misspelled in the manuscript.
[10] That is: "We magnify you," which is the Introduction to the Creed.

of the Angels, the Trisagion, and the rest. At the end of reciting the Creed, they light up candles... etc.

The *Manuscript of the Hanging Church Typikon (16th century)* reads:

> They start the Matins Prayer as usual after having adorned the Cross with olive and palm branches and a green silk cloth or the likes of. After the Praise of the Angles and the Creed, the priest takes this Cross and raises it saying ⲫϯ ⲛⲁⲓ ⲛⲁⲛ etc.

The *Manuscript of the Haret Zuweila Typikon (17th century)* mentions the following:

> ... after the Praise of the Angels, they say the Doxologies... then the Creed...

The *Manuscript of the London Typikon* indicates that they ...

> start the Matins Prayer as usual, then raise incense. As the priest circles around with incense, they adorn a cross with olive and palm branches and wrap it in a green cloth or another. They also distribute woven olive and palm branches, as well as candles, to the congregation. After the Praise of the Angels, they say the Doxology of the feast, followed by the Creed. Then, the priest raises the aforementioned Cross of olives and says ⲫϯ ⲛⲁⲓ ⲛⲁⲛ, and the congregation reply with Kyrie eleison in the Great Tune...

Section Two: The Rite of the Hosanna Procession in the Matins Raising of Incense

First: Ibn Kabar

In the *Manuscript of Paris* and the *Manuscript of Uppsala*:[11]

> ... they take up the olive, which is made of olive and palm branches and adorned with patterns,[12] and encircle the church with it while carrying crosses, candles and censers[13] before it, and they stop before the sanctuaries and the places of the icons.
>
> In each of these stations, they read the Psalm and the Gospel[14] in Coptic,[15] followed by a part of the Commentary of the feast, and they chant[16] with the Tune of the Cross.
>
> Some people practice this after the Prayer[17] of the Psalmody, before the Matins Prayer, while others practice it after the Matins Prayer and Raising of Incense, before the Gospel Reading.
>
> The Gospel Readings read during the procession around the Church with the olive branches depend on the custom of every church.

---

[11] with some corrections in the spelling and dividing the text into paragraphs.
[12] "adorned with patterns" means warped in cloths
[13] *Manuscript of Paris*: - censers
[14] *Manuscript of Uppsala*: a Gospel
[15] *Manuscript of Paris*: and then in Arabic
[16] *Manuscript of Uppsala*: respond
[17] *Manuscript of Uppsala*: - prayer

In the Hanging Church in Cairo, they usually read before the icon[18] of Palm Sunday, the pericope about Zacchaeus the tax collector from Luke;[19] before the icon of St. George,[20] the passage about the End;[21] before the sanctuary of John the Baptist, they read the passage pertaining to his account and praise;[22] before the women's chorus, the passage about the centurion[23] from Luke;[24] before the icon[25] of the Lady,[26] the passage about the annunciation from Luke; before the sanctuary of Michael,[27] the section about the merchant from Matthew;[28] before the baptismal font, they read[29] the passage from Luke 'and Mary arose.'[30]

---

[18] *Uppsala*: icon
[19] Luke 19:1-10
[20] *Manuscript of Uppsala*: saint
[21] probably Matthew 24 or Mark 13 or Luke 21
[22] probably Matthew 11 or Luke 7
[23] *Uppsala*: "And while they are walking" instead of "the part about the centurion."
[24] Luke 7:1-10
[25] *Uppsala*: icon
[26] Luke 1:26-38
[27] *Paris*: "Mikaeel"
[28] Matthew 13:44-52
[29] *Uppsala*: it is read
[30] *Uppsala*: ... baptismal font, 'In those days Mary arose' from Luke.
Luke 1:39-56
It is quite perplexing that this part is read before the baptismal font, since John was baptised with the Holy Spirit in his mother's womb when St. Mary the Virgin greeted Elizabeth. For "when Elizabeth heard the greeting of Mary, the babe leaped in her womb; and Elizabeth was filled with the Holy Spirit."

In the *Manuscript of Paris*: The practice of the monks in the Shahran[31] Monastery is that they read the passage appropriate for every icon they stand before and every place they proceed to within the monastery. Thus, before the sanctuaries they read passages that mention the temple, before icons they read what corresponds to each of them, by the mill and the bakery the passage about the yeast, by the table and the sacristy the pericopes about the five loaves and the seven loaves of bread, by the well the passages pertaining to the Samaritan women, and at the cemetery the passages about the deceased, depending on each one which are mentioned in the Funeral Book.

The Order practiced in the monasteries[32] of St. Macarius depends on what they see fit as they proceed with the olive branch around the monastery, inside and outside.

The people of Upper Egypt have their own *harmonies*[33]

---

[31] Shahran is now the winepress and the monastery of Abba Parsoma the Naked. It lies on the road leading from Tora to Atfih (Giza Governorate). Shahran was a large, inhabited village by the banks of the river (the Nile). It is said that Moses the prophet was born there, and it was from there that his mother put him in a basket in the Nile. It is a sought-after coveted location due to its proximity to Cairo. Opposite of this monastery, in the southern mountain, lies a large cave etched by columns as a house inside the mountain. It is so great that it is known by the appellation of "the city."
The Shahran Monastery was renovated by Poemen the monk in the times of Imam the ruler. This monk was the reason churches reopened and the caliph's orders which lasted for nine years were repealed. Pope Zechariah, the 64th Patriarch, was arrested in this monastery and cast to the lions, but they did not harm him, for God prevented the lions from approaching him because of his righteousness and strong faith in the Lord. The monastery also included a palace with a garden, which was linked to the monastery. The monastery extended over six acres, which included fruitful palms and farmlands. Imam the caliph resided in the garden of this monastery and took strolls in it. From there, he used to go out into the mountain and meander through the wilderness.
From the book of Abu Almakarem (mistakenly attributed to Abu Saleh the Armenian), *The History of the Churches and Monasteries in the Twelfth Century*, Volume 2, 83-84.
[32] It is not clear whether the author meant Macarius' Monastery alone or all the monasteries of the Natron Valley. It is also unknown whether he was referring to written traditions or unrecorded liturgical customs that were passed on.
Wadi the Franciscan, *op. cit.*, Volume 34, 296.
[33] The author may be referring to the plural of the word "harmony," meaning musical consistency.
A few years later, I learned that George Philotheos Awad has explained it in a footnote as: "Harmonice, a Greek word ⲁⲣⲙⲟⲛⲓⲁⲥ meaning orderly tunes, consistent voices, congruent melodies." Wadi the Franciscan, *op. cit.*, Volume 34, 297.

and dogmas³⁴ that are derived from the Psalms of David, which are recorded in their Typikon -called "The Kovos."³⁵ They select from these what they see fit to pray and chant in good long tunes in every place they

---

According to two recent studies:
John Drescher, *The Earliest Biblical Concordances*, Bulletin de la société d'archéologie Copte 15 (1958-1960), 63-67; Hans Queck, *Untersuchungen zum koptischen stundengebet* (Louvain, 1970), 97-104,
there is a book titled ϨⲈⲢⲘⲎⲚⲒⲀ in the Manuscript of Pierpont Morgan M 574 in the White Monastery near Sohag, which goes back to the year 895 AD. This manuscript is made up of verses from the Book of Psalms that pertain to the same subject or word. Thus, the word may mean an interpretation of the Psalm in the form of a collocation.
Refer to: Franciscan Brother Wadi, *op. cit.*, Volume 34, 296.
³⁴ He possibly means the plural of the word "dogma," meaning canon or doctrine.
A few years later, I learned that Jirjis Philotheos Awad has explained it in a footnote as: "Dogmas comes from the Greek word ⲦⲀⲄⲘⲀⲦⲞⲤ meaning order, consistency, system." Thus, we can deduce that "dogmas" here also refers to a collection of verses from the Psalms that cover some thematic topics δόγματα associated with prophecies about Christ, the Virgin Mary, the Resurrection, and others.
Wadi the Franciscan, *op. cit.*, Volume 34, 297.
³⁵ I do not know the meaning of this word. Jirjis Philotheos Awad wrote it as "The Logos" and explained it in a footnote as: The Logos in Greek ⲖⲞⲄⲞⲤ means book." However, one cannot accept this reading as the letter "K" is very clear in all the manuscripts. Yet, neither myself nor the people I asked, who are knowledgeable in the Coptic language and rite, were able to decipher the meaning of this word. Perhaps the Coptic word was ⲔⲞⲢⲞⲤ or ⲬⲞⲢⲞⲤ meaning chorus or circle, because the text was read in the form of a chorus or in the form of connected circles, while the author misspelled the letter ⲣ as ⲫ.
Wadi the Francisca, *op. cit.*, Volume 34, 297-298.

pass by or before everything they go before, whether see, sand, mountain, grass, tree or else.

In the *Manuscript of Paris* and the *Manuscript of Uppsala*: "Then, it is customary for the Egyptians[36] to return with the olive back to the sanctuary."

Commentary on Ibn Kabar's recount of the Hosanna Procession

- Despite the differences that Ibn Kabar details with respect to the Hosanna Procession between churches and regions, they all seem to coincide on reading a relevant Gospel passage then chanting an appropriate response at different stations during the procession.

- During the thirteenth century, or perhaps just prior to it, the ritual of the Hosanna Procession proliferated in the Church in the manner of its earlier known observance in the two Feasts of the Cross. However, every church practiced it in accordance with its own customs. Some churches conducted this stational procession after the Midnight and Lauds Praises but before the Matins Raising of Incense, while others

---

[36] *Uppsala*: It is customary for the Egyptians…
The author may be referring here to the residents of Old Cairo, where the Hanging Church of St. Mary is located.

conducted it during the Matins Raising of Incense before the Gospel Reading.

- The Hosanna Procession was performed inside as well as outside the church building, not only in the monasteries, but also in the cities. In the earlier days, the Procession of the Cross was held outside the church in the monasteries as well as the cities, as mentioned by Fr Louis Villecourt.[37] Then, in the cities, it was confined to inside the church only, which Ibn Kabar mentioned about the Hanging Church of St. Mary in Old Cairo, but continued to be held inside and outside the monastery complexes for a long time until very recently.[38] I will speak on this later.

- At each station of the procession, they read the suitable Psalm and Gospel Reading according to the custom of each church, as well as part of the Commentary of the Feast "Ascend to the high mountains...," followed by the Hosanna Response in the Tune of the Cross. It is obvious here that there is no allusion to repeating the

---

[37] Dom Louis Villecourt, *Les observances liturgiques et la discipline du jeûne dans l'Eglise Copte* (Le Muséon: revue d'études orientales 37 (1924)); Gérard Viaud, *La procession des deux fêtes de la croix et du dimanche des rameaux dans l'Eglise Copte*, BSAC, 19, 212.
[38] Gérard Viaud, *op. cit.*, 214.

Litany of the Gospel before each of these Gospel Readings.[39]

- There is no specification of the number of Gospel Readings that are read during the Hosanna Procession as it depends on the custom of each church.

- The custom in Upper Egypt regarding the liturgical elements of the Hosanna Procession differs from that in Old Cairo, Lower Egypt, and the monasteries.

Second: Ibn Sebā'

... As for the procession with the olive branch that the people celebrate today, they proceed with it inside the monasteries, the mill, the sacristy,[40] outside the monastery, the claustral prior's office, and every place. This practice is not appropriate on Palm Sunday, but only on the Feasts of the Cross for receiving the blessing of the cross. The procession on Palm Sunday should only be around the four corners of the church in the shape of the cross.[41]

---

[39] This is mentioned in the book of *The Order of the Procession of the Two Feasts of the Cross and Palm Sunday*...
[40] Written differently in the Arabic text.
[41] Yoḥanna Ibn Zakaria Ibn Sebā', *op. cit.*, 320.

Commentary on Ibn Sebā's recount of the Hosanna Procession

It is also evident, from Ibn Sebā's account, that the Hosanna Procession, which was introduced into the rite during the Middle Ages was patterned in accordance with that of the Feasts of the Cross. This rite first appeared in the monasteries before it became known in the urban rite.

Third: Church Order Manuscript No. 118 (Rites) in Cairo Patriarchate of 1911

The manuscript reads: In this respect, they prepare[42] the cross, which is made of olive and palm branches, and shroud it in a green silk cloth, if available, or the likes of. The priests take up censers and crosses in their hands, and candles are lit. They also distribute[43] olive and palm branches to the congregation like the Hebrew children who went ahead of Christ. After reciting the Creed, the priest takes up the aforementioned olive cross, lifts it up and says Ⲫ︦ϯ ⲛⲁⲓ ⲛⲁⲛ, while they respond[44] with Kyrie eleison in the Great Tune. Then, they circumambulate the altar[45] with the cross three[46] times and then

---

[42] Written differently in the Arabic text.
[43] Written differently in the Arabic text.
[44] Written differently in the Arabic text.
[45] Written differently in the Arabic text.
[46] Written differently in the Arabic text.

descend[47] to the chorus while chanting[48] the Hymn of Ⲉⲩⲗⲟⲅⲏⲙⲉⲛⲟⲥ. Afterwards, they recite the Commentary in the tune of the feast. They proceed[49] around, each church according to its own custom, patterned after the procession on the Feasts of the Cross. When they arrive at the first place, they respond[50] saying ·Ⲱⲥⲁⲛⲛⲁ ϧⲉⲛ ⲛⲏⲉⲧϭⲟⲥⲓ ..., then the officiating priest proceeds to recite the Litany of the Gospel, followed by the Psalm and its response,[51] and the Gospel in both Coptic and Arabic. They respond with the first Hosanna tune and the Commentary. The Hosanna is chanted without hymn[52] as they walk to the next station. They continue[53] in this manner for the entire rite of the Procession until they return to the chorus.

Fourth: The Other Manuscripts under Study
The *Manuscript of Abba Shenoute Typikon (15th century)* reads:

> ... After reciting the Creed, they light up candles, and the priests and deacons each take up olive and palm branches in their hands. The priest lifts the cross and says Ⲫϯ ⲛⲁⲓ ⲛⲁⲛ

---

[47] Written differently in the Arabic text.
[48] Written differently in the Arabic text.
[49] Written differently in the Arabic text.
[50] Written differently in the Arabic text.
[51] Written differently in the Arabic text.
[52] Written differently in the Arabic text.
[53] Written differently in the Arabic text.

> as usual, and the deacons chant Kyrie eleison in the Great Tune while they circumambulate the altar three times, raising the cross and the Gospel. They, then descend to the chorus and chant the Hosanna Hymn of Ⲉⲩⲗⲟⲅⲏⲙⲉⲛⲟⲥ before the cross. Afterwards, they recite one verse of the Hosanna in the Tune of the Cross and circle the church once with the Cross, each church according to its own custom with respect to its stations, while chanting the Commentary. At each of the stations, the priest starts with the Gospel passage in Coptic and Arabic, and they respond with the Hosanna one word with hymn, followed by the Commentary. They continue in this manner until the Procession's prayers and Gospels are completed, and they return to the chorus and the priest says the Litany of the Gospel. Then, they proceed with the Matins Psalm and Gospel Reading...

Virtually the same order is mentioned in the other manuscripts under study.

The *Manuscript of the Hanging Church Typikon (16th century)* reads:

> ... and they circle around the church in accordance with its own custom and the known places in the Hosanna Procession...[54]

The *Manuscript of London Typikon* reads:

---

[54] The same is mentioned in the *Manuscript of Haret Zuweila Typikon (17th century)*.

... as they walk around the church, each according to its own custom for the Cross Procession...

Commentary on the Contemporary Hosanna Procession in the Matins Prayer

The reader may be surprised to know that the published liturgical books that are currently used by the Church do not conform to what was mentioned in the Church Order manuscripts or the other manuscripts under study. Rather, each book seems to include a somewhat different rite in some of its aspects in contrast to what other books mentioned.

For example, when *The Typikon and Order of the Passion Week and the Glorious Passover Feast (1920)* speaks of the Hosanna Procession in page 82, it says:

> They prepare a cross of palm and olive branches[55] in the likeness of the Hebrew children who walked before Christ.

Then, the Typikon mentions: "The priest takes up the cross and lifts it up, saying..." Here, also, the Typikon ignores the expression "the aforementioned olive cross" which is mentioned in the Church Order manuscript, as well as in the other manuscripts. That is to say, when the

---

[55] Here the Guide fails to mention the detail: "they wrap it in a green silk cloth, if available, or the likes of. The priests take up censers and crosses in their hands, the candles are lit, and they distribute olive and palm branches among the congregation."

priest says Ⲫϯ ⲛⲁⲓ ⲛⲁⲛ "Lord have Mercy," he holds up the cross that is made up of olive and palm branches, and not any other cross.

The Typikon also stipulates that: "Afterwards, they circle around the altar three times..." Here, also, the Guide has reduced the expression "they circle with the cross around the altar three times." That is to say, circling the altar in the sanctuary is done while holding up the olive cross that is made up of olive and palm branches and covered in a green silk cloth, or of a similar fabric.

The Typikon mentions that after the priest says Ⲫϯ ⲛⲁⲓ ⲛⲁⲛ, that is "God have Mercy," the congregation responds with Kyrie eleison three times, and then circle the altar three times while chanting Kyrie eleison. However, the Church Order manuscripts, along with the other manuscripts under study, state that, after the priest says, "Lord have Mercy," they respond with Kyrie eleison in the Great Tune while they circumambulate with the olive cross around the altar three times.

Both the Typikon and all the manuscripts agree that after the procession around the altar three times is complete, they stand before the door of the sanctuary and chant the Hosanna Hymn of Ⲉⲩⲗⲟⲅⲏⲙⲉⲛⲟⲥ and then recite the Commentary of Palm Sunday.

However, from this point, the Typikon greatly deviates from the manuscripts. Whereas the Church Order manuscripts, and the other manuscripts under study, state that "the Commentary is read with the tune of the feast while they proceed around the church, each one in accordance with its own custom, which borrows its order from the Feast of the Cross," the Typikon indicates that "they circle around the church, and the priest raises incense before the altars and the icons, while they recite antiphons pertaining to the Procession, which are also chanted during the two Feasts of the Cross."

The difference between the Church Order manuscripts and the Typikon is significant. The manuscripts mention that the Hosanna Procession is about moving from one place to another, and not merely moving from one icon inside the church to another icon. I will explain this in greater detail later.

Furthermore, it is quite noticeable that the manuscripts confirm that the Hosanna Procession is performed according to the custom of each church, which is the same custom the church has for the Feast of the Cross. In other words, the Procession of the Feast of the Cross is the original source from which the Feast of Palm Sunday derives its own ceremonial procession. The same is confirmed by Ibn Sebā, as previously noted.

These are the main differences between what the manuscripts mention and what came in *The Typikon and Order of the Passion Week and the Glorious Passover Feast (1920)*.[56]

The Order of the Procession of the Two Feasts of the Cross and Palm Sunday, and the Commentaries of the Great Lent and Eastertide according to the Rite of the Coptic Orthodox Church[57] includes a different ritual compared to what appeared in the Typikon regarding the Hosanna Procession. It states in page 3 and afterwards the following:

> When the priest lifts the cross and says Ⲫϯ ⲛⲁⲓ ⲛⲁⲛ the chanters respond saying = Ⲕⲉ three times with the cymbals... If it was Palm Sunday, they chant the Hymn of Ⲉⲩⲗⲟⲅⲏⲙⲉⲛⲟⲥ before the Procession of the Cross. Then, they say the Commentary of the blessed Palm Sunday 'Ascend to the high mountains...'... Then the priest says the Litany of the Gospel, and they recite the Psalm without hymn before the main altar...[58]

Then on page 51, titled "The How of the Procession of the Cross," it also mentions:

---

[56] What is quite remarkable is that the time gap between what came in the *Church Order Manuscript No. 118 (Rites) in Cairo Patriarchate 1911* and what is mentioned in the Guide does not exceed ten years!
[57] Published
[58] This is the Psalm of the first Gospel of the twelves Gospel Readings that are read in the Procession.

> They enter the sanctuary and circle the altar three times, then descend and circle the nave three times, and return to the sanctuary and circle the altar once, then exit the sanctuary, where the priest says the Litany of the Gospel, and they read the Matins Psalm as usual.

It is clear here that, according to Book of the Procession of the Two Feasts of the Cross and Palm Sunday, after the priest says Ⲱⲧ ⲛⲁⲓ ⲛⲁⲛ, they say Kyrie eleison three times in the Great Tune, followed by the Hosanna Hymn and the Commentary. Afterwards, they read the twelve Gospel Readings around the church, and then enter the sanctuary and circle around the altar three times. Then they circle around the nave three times and return to the sanctuary to circumambulate the altar once more. Then the priest prays the Litany of the Gospel and they read the Matins Gospel excerpt of the feast.

Thus, while the Typikon specifies three circumambulations around the altar before the Hosanna Hymn and twelve Gospel Readings around the church, the book of the Procession of the Two Feasts of the Cross and Palm Sunday specifies a total of seven revolutions around the altar and the nave after the Hosanna Hymn and the twelve Gospel Readings around the church.

This latter rite is not mentioned in any Church Order manuscript or in the other manuscripts under study, as pointed out by O.H.E. Burmester, who specifies -

without detailed research- that the Hosanna Procession is performed after the twelve Gospel Readings.[59]

Documentary Certificate on the Hosanna Procession in the mid fourteenth century

We have documentation on the Hosanna Procession in St. Macarius Monastery, which dates to the mid fourteenth century, during the time of Pope Peter V (1340 – 1348), the 83rd Patriarch, particularly when he officiated the consecration of the Holy Chrism in the aforementioned monastery in 1340 AD. Accordingly, we read the following in the Manuscript No. 100 (Arabic), currently kept at the National Library in Paris:

> In the early morning of the day, after the Midnight Prayer, the monk fathers, the monastery priest, prayed the Matins Prayer. The prayer was officiated by Anba Gabriel, the Bishop of Taḥa. They raised incense and recited the doxology. Then, the pope arrived, wearing a green vestment, with the rest of the bishops, and they recited the Praise of the Angels until the end.
>
> Then, they exited the church, and the pope mounted his colt while wearing his vestment and escorted by an entourage of bishops, monks and laymen on foot. They carried olive and palm branches in their hands with lit candles, raised Gospels, ringing bells, and the pattern raised on his head as at first. The priests, certain that Christ

---

[59] Oswald H.E. KHS-Burmester, *The Egyptian or Coptic Church, op. cit.*, 268.

was in their midst, cried out saying: "Hosanna in the highest; blessed is He who comes in the name of the Lord."

They continued to circumambulate the monastery fortress, while continuing with the Readings and Commentaries until they reached the saintly patriarch and fathers where they offered a prayer. Then they went to the cave tomb of the saintly monks Abba Abram and George, where the pope dismounted his ride and prayed the Funeral Prayer. Afterwards, he mounted his ride again, surrounded by the assembly on foot, who continued the Readings until they entered the church. Then they continued the prayer as usual.

It is obvious, here, that the Matins Hosanna Procession is not confined within the church walls, but extends to the outside as well, passing by places that are specific to each church or monastery. This practice continued throughout the following centuries until the beginning of the twentieth century, when the book of the Palm Sunday Procession was published in 1921. It both confined the procession within the church walls and curtailed it to a great extent, standardizing specific saints' icons on every church and neglecting holy sites specific to individual churches and monasteries, as well as the vast diversity of icons and relics of martyrs and saints in these churches. O how many are the saints? Who can count their number? For they are as many as the crops of the fields, as the books say!

Documentary Certificate on the Hosanna Procession in the nineteenth century

There are two manuscripts before us:

The first manuscript is from Al-Baramūs Monastery of the Virgin Lady in the Natron Valley, which is numbered 133 (Rite) and is titled "The Procession Gospels and the Pascha Commentaries and Psalms." Although it is not dated, we can deduce the date of its transcription to extend to the nineteenth century like many of the manuscripts kept in this monastery.[60] The manuscript includes sixteen Gospel Pericopes that are read inside the church and around the monastery during the Procession of Palm Sunday and the two Feasts of the Cross.

The second manuscript is from Al-Muharraq Monastery of the Virgin Lady, which is numbered (13D S 19 Rite). It is not dated and contains thirteen Gospels that are either read inside or outside the church during the Procession of the two Feasts of the Cross or Palm Sunday.

The following table illustrates the differences between these two manuscripts and compares those to the current practice according to the published book of the Procession of the Two Feasts of the Cross and Palm Sunday.

---

[60] Gérard Viaud, *op. cit.*, 212.

Station	Al-Baramus monastery	Al-Muharraq Monastery	Current Practice
One	In front of the sanctuary Psalm 44:15[61] Luke 10:38-42	In front of the sanctuary Psalm 137:1-2 John 2:13-25	In front of the main sanctuary[62] Psalm 103:4, 137:1 John 1:44-52
Two	St. Moses[63] and all the saints Psalm 4:3-4 Matthew 16:24-28	Outer Chorus Psalm 92:4-5 Matthew 2:13-22	In front of the icon of St. Mary Psalm 86:2,5,7 Luke 1:39-56
Three	Prince Theodore of Shotep[64] Psalm 33:67 Luke 12:4-12	In front of the icon of St. Mary Psalm 44:9-10 Luke 1:39-56	In front of the icon of Archangel Gabriel[65] Psalm 33:6-8 Luke 1:26-38

---

[61] The psalm numbers mentioned here are according to the Septuagint Translation.
[62] The first station in the Hanging Church is in front of the Palm Sunday icon, where they read Luke 19:1-10.
[63] The relics of St. Moses are kept in the northern part of the outer chorus, which is the chorus of the monks.
[64] Shotep lies in the southeastern part of Asyūṭ Governorate, and it was built by King Mancaus.
[65] In the Hanging Church, they read Luke 1:26-38 in front of the Annunciation icon for the fifth station of the procession.

Four	St. Georgy the Martyr Psalm 112:1 Luke 21:12-19	Icon of the twelve apostles Psalm 18:4 Matthew 10:1-8	Icon of Archangel Michael[66] Psalm 102:17-18 Matthew 13:44-52
Five	At the table[67] Psalm 149:1 Luke 9:12-17	In front of the Cross Psalm 59:4-5 Matthew 16:24-28	In front of the icon of St. Mark the Apostle Psalm 67:13 Luke 10:1-12
Six	For the departed[68] Psalm 44:15 Matthew 22:23-33	In front of the baptismal font[69] Psalm 31:1-2 John 3:3-6	In front of the icon of the apostles Psalm 18:3-4 Matthew 10:1-8

---

[66] In the Hanging Church, they read Matthew 13:44-52 in front of the icon of Archangel Michael for the sixths station.

[67] In Shahran Monastery, they read the Gospels of the five loaves and the seven loaves at the table (Matthew 14:15-21), (Mark 6:30-44), (Luke 9:10-17), (John 6:1-14), (Matthew 15:32-39), (Mark 8:1-10).

[68] The tombs are located at the southwestern corner of the monastery. In Shahran Monastery they read some excerpts from the Funeral Book (Le livre des obsèques) at the tombs.

[69] In the Hanging Church, Luke 1:39 is read in front of the baptismal font for the seventh station of the procession.

Seven	St. Apollo and St. Abib[70] Psalm 11:5 Matthew 24:42-47	In the church of St. George Psalm 36:39-40 Matthew 10:26-33	In front of the icon of St. George[71] Psalm 96:11 Luke 21:12-19
Eight	By the sacristy[72] Psalm 92:1 Luke 13:17-21	In the Church of St. John the Baptist Psalm 91:12-13 Mark 1:1-11	In front of the icon of St. Antony Psalm 67:33, 4 Matthew 16:24-28
Nine	By the waterwheel or the water spring[73] Psalm 97:2 John 4:1-14	By the tomb of Moses[74] Psalm 117:19-20 Mark 6:1-16	In front of the northern door Psalm 83:1-2 Luke 13:22-30

---

[70] This icon still exists in the church of the monastery, but certainly not in the same location it stood during the transcription of the manuscript.

[71] In the Hanging Church, they read Matthew 24:3, Mark 13:3 or Luke 21:5 in front of the icon of St. George for the second station of the procession.

[72] That is by the storage room of the monastery. In Shahran Monastery, they read the Gospels of the five loaves or the seven loaves both at the table and by the sacristy.

[73] In Shahran Monastery, they read the part about the Samaritan woman from John 4 by the well.

[74] Moses is a descendant of the tribe of Judah, who was related to St. Joseph the Carpenter. He died in Koskam (Al-Muharraq Monastery) during the time the Holy Family visited Egypt.

Ten	By St. John the Baptist Psalm 41:8 3:1-17	At the table Psalm 110:4-5 Matthew 14:15-21	By the font towards the church south Psalm 28:3-4 Matthew 3:13-17
Eleven	In the garden[75] Psalm 103:15 13:24-30	By the well Psalm 64:9 John 4:6-11	In front of the southern door Psalm 117:19-20 Matthew 21:1-11
Twelve	By the mill[76] Psalm 4:3-4 Matthew 24:40-44	In the garden Psalm 64:10-11 Matthew 20:1-15	Icon of St. John the Baptist[77] Psalm 51:7-8 Matthew 7:28-35
Thirteen	By the palace Psalm 76:15 Matthew 24:26-39	In front of the icon of Archangel Michael Psalm 147:1-2	

---

[75] The monastery has two gardens, one in the middle of the monks' cells and the other along the southern wall of the monastery.

[76] The mill lies to the north of the church, close to the palace. In Shahran Monastery they read the part about the yeast by the mill and the baker (Matthew 13:33, Luke 13:20).

[77] In the Hanging Church, the passage read in front of the sanctuary of St. John the Baptist is Matthew 11:2, Luke 7:18.

		Matthew 13:33-52	
Fourteen	St. Parsoma the Naked[78] Psalm 112:1 Luke 21:12-19		
Fifteen	St. Antony Psalm 91:8 Luke 19:11-19		
Sixteen	St. Maximus and St. Domatiums Psalm 72:23-24 Matthew 5:3-16		

It is important to note here that the fourth Gospel that is read in the Hanging Church in the women's chorus, which is from Luke 7:1, does not have a counterpart in the other celebrations of the Hosanna and the Cross Procession.

Thus, until the end of the nineteenth century and the beginning of the twentieth century the Hosanna Procession was not uniform in all churches and monasteries. However, when the book of the Hosanna

---

[78] At this station, the Hosanna Procession returns to the church, stopping by some of the icons of saints.

Procession was published in 1921, the procession was standardized all over the churches, and in the monasteries as well after some time. Yet, it remains difficult to date when the readings of the Gosels became association with specific saints and their icons. Hence, it is illogical to deduce that the order of the icons of the saints on the iconostasis is subject to the order that came in the book of the Cross and Hosanna Procession.

In fact, publishing a book that unites the rite of the Cross and Hosanna Procession across all churches and monasteries has resulted in the loss of a rich liturgical diversity that the Coptic Church knew for many centuries from the far north to the south. The wealth of the Church in its innumerable saints cannot be limited to the ten saints that are now honoured in every church and monastery.[79]

---

[79] Note, for example, how difficult it became to perform the Hosanna or Cross Procession in its current form in the church of St. Macarius in his monastery in Scetis, where the iconostasis only includes a handful of saints, among whom is the icon of the three saintly youth. Furthermore, the icon of St. John the Baptist lies in the far northern part of the church in accordance with an ancient tradition in the monastery. Yet, we are compelled to adhere to this recent rite that diverges from the monastery's original rite.
It is important to note here that when Pope Shenouda III visited the monastery in May 2009, he decided to have a new iconostasis designed for the church of St. Macarius that befits the monastery and its main church. He assigned this task to specialists in this matter.

The Processions for the Feast of the Cross, and Palm Sunday in which the Cross is carried, are a source of blessing for the different parts of the church or the monastery because of the blessing of the glorious Cross and the readings of the Holy Gospel.

Gérard Viaud wonders here: What is the origin of this procession? Is it a patrimony of ancient processions that were known in Pharaonic Egypt? Pharaonic priests were accustomed to cruising the River Nile in a boat with a statue of a god kept in a wooden microcosm of a miniature temple and stopping at particular stations near the villages, they would carry the statue on their shoulders, make offerings, raise incense, and proclaim readings.

These processions were dedicated to particular important events throughout the year, like the flooding of the Nile, the feast of harvest, the feast of one of the gods, etc.

It is important to note here that participating in a procession to procure the blessing of the gods is not a unique Egyptian custom, for the Greek Church practices a procession called λιτανια (Litania) while carrying icons and stopping at a number of stations where they pray for the head of the church, the priestly orders, the king and the government, the city and its inhabitants, and the fruits of the earth.

Furthermore, the Western Church also knows such processions, where the ceremonial procession in the Latin Rite takes place on April 25th every year, which marks the start of the harvesting season.

Thus, the main idea of these processions is to seek the protection of the god or gods and to plead for their divine blessing to rest on the plantation, cities, seas, elements of nature, and man's needs.[80]

Accordingly, the Coptic Tradition coincides with that of other churches, but profoundly captures in sacramental form the importance of turning to the Almighty God and seeking His protection, help and blessing with the power of the Holy Cross, the source of all blessings.

Section Three: The Rite of what follows the Hosanna Procession until the End of the Prayers of the Matins Raising of Incense

Ibn Kabar

The *Manuscript of Paris* and the *Manuscript of Uppsala* state the following:

---

[80] Gérard Viaud, *op. cit.*, 223-224.

They pray the Litany of the Gospel, followed by the Psalm and Gospel Reading.[81] Then, they continue the prayer and commence the Liturgy Service...

The Other Manuscripts under Study

The *Manuscript of Abba Shenoute Typikon (14th century)* reads:

> Then they return to the chorus and the priest prays the Litany of the Gospel followed by the Psalm of the Matins Prayer and the Gospel Reading. They respond with `Ⲧⲫⲁϣⲓ ⲛ̀ⲛⲓⲁ̀ⲣⲭⲱⲛⲧⲁ`[82] and continue the Matins Prayer as usual. They recite the canon that is first mentioned in the Vespers Prayer and conclude the prayer with the priest reciting the benediction. Then they begin the sanctification of the oblations as usual...

The *Manuscript of the Hanging Church Typikon (16th century)* includes the following:

> ... When they return to the chorus, they read the Litany of the Gospel and respond saying... then continue the prayer as usual. They recite the canon that suits the feast and begin the Liturgy Service as usual...

The *Church Order Manuscript No. 118 (Rites) in Cairo Patriarchate for the year 1911* reads:

---

[81] *Uppsala*: Reading from the Gospel of Luke.
[82] The manuscript includes the full text in both Coptic and Arabic. It also includes another response.

The serving priest prays the Litany of the Matins Gospel in front of the sanctuary, then they chant the Psalm and respond as usual. They read the Gospel and respond with Ṯϥⲁϣⲓ ⲛ̀ⲛⲓϩⲩⲡⲁⲣⲭⲱⲛⲧⲁ then Ⲩⲥ ⲡⲓⲟⲩⲝⲁⲓ ⲁϥϣⲱⲡⲓ ⲛⲉⲙⲁϥ as in the third Sunday of the month of Thout. Then, they continue[83] the prayer as usual. They read the canon of Ⲣⲁϣⲓ ⲟⲩⲛⲟϥ Ⲥⲓⲱⲛ as in the Vespers Prayer, and the priest recites the benediction. Praise be to God forever.

The Matins Psalm Versicle is from Psalm 67:19,35:

The God of Israel, He gives power and strength[84] to His people. Blessed be the Lord. Alleluia.

The Gospel is from Luke 19:1-10 about the Lord's invitation of Zacchaeus, the chief tax collector who was seeking to behold Jesus for salvation.

The Gospel Response corresponds to the Gospel Reading whose events take place in Jericho, the last city Jesus passed by before entering Jerusalem.

---

[83] Written differently in the Arabic text.
[84] It means majesty and dominion. It is sometimes mistranslated, as is sometimes done in the Paschal Prayer of "Yours is the power, the glory, the blessing and majesty," to richness and supremacy, which is incorrect. Other Church Readings render it as "solace and comfort," which is also incorrect, as appeared in the Vesperal Psalm Versicle of 14 Paopi, the Matins Psalm Versicle of 25 Hathor, the Liturgy Psalm Versicle of 27 Pharmuthi, and the Vesperal Psalm Versicle of 26 Pashons.

The response reads:

> Zacchaeus said to his Lord, 'Half of my goods I will give, O Master, to the poor with diligence.' The Lord God of powers said, 'Behold salvation has come unto you today, for you are also a son of Abraham.'

The prayers of the Matins Raising of Incense are concluded as usual.

Chapter Five: The Rite of Palm Sunday Liturgy Service

First: According to the Manuscripts and the Liturgical References

1. Ibn Kabar

The *Manuscript of Paris* and the *Manuscript of Uppsala* state the following:

> And they start the Liturgy Service, not the one according to St. Cyril, but either that of St. Gregory or St. Basil,[1] preferably of St. Gregory as it is specific to the Lordly Feasts and divine joys.[2]

2. Ibn Sebā'

> At the time of the Liturgy Service, the patriarch ascends to commence the service, for this is a Lordly Feast. And at the time of the Gospel Reading, the priests take the olive cross to the East into the *Thronos*.[3] The Psalm is recited in the Sinjārī Tune, then the patriarch reads the Gospel passage from Matthew, which is the first of the four Gospel

---

[1] "They pray the Liturgy of either St. Gregory or St. Basil according to the custom of every church."
Cf. Oswald H.E. KHS-Burmester, *The Egyptian or Coptic Church, op. cit.*, 273.

[2] *Uppsala*: includes some minor differences.

[3] "Thronos" is a Coptic word, meaning throne. It refers to the bishop's ceremonial seat which was situated at the eastern end of the main sanctuary on the stairs. Our Coptic manuscripts include this Coptic word in various transliterations, namely "the Setras," "the Setrans," "the Setronos."

pericopes. Afterwards, the patriarch and the priests take the olive cross and proceed to the western end of the church, where they recite another Psalm and the patriarch reads the Gospel Reading from Mark. Then, they chant before the olive cross while the priests walk towards the northern end of the church, where the Patriarch recites the Litany of the Gospel, and they recite another Psalm and the Gospel Reading from Luke. Afterwards, they chant while proceeding to the southern end of the church, where the Patriarch recites the Litany of the Gospel, and they recite the Psalm and the Gospel Reading from John.[4]

When they finish reading the four Gospel Readings in the four corners of the church in the shape of the cross, they distribute it[5] to the congregation, each one according to his or her needs, and they hang the remains above the pulpit.

With respect to the procession with the olive cross, which the people practice today in the monasteries where they proceed around to the mill, the sacristy, outside the monastery, to the claustral prior's office, and every other place, it ought not happen on Palm Sunday, but only on the Feast of the Cross for receiving the cross' blessing. The olive cross should only be moved around the four corners of the church in the shape of a cross.[6]

Commentary on what came in Ibn Sebā' about the Liturgy Service of Palm Sunday

What came in the last two paragraphs by Ibn Sebā' is the old rite of reading the four Gospels during the

---

[4] Yoḥanna Ibn Zakaria Ibn Sebā', *op. cit.*, 319-320.
[5] That is the olive cross.
[6] Yoḥanna Ibn Zakaria Ibn Sebā', *op. cit.*, 320-321.

Liturgy Service of Palm Sunday, especially in the churches of Upper Egypt. In each of the four readings they pray the following liturgical elements: The Litany of the Gospel, some verses from the Psalms, then the Gospel Reading, followed by a chant which may be the Gospel Response. The latter is what Ibn Sebā' refers to by saying:

> ...they chant before the olive cross while the priests walk towards... the Gospel Reading from Luke. Afterwards, they walk while chanting...

3. The Church Order Manuscript No. 118 (Rites) in Cairo Patriarchate for the year 1911

This manuscript[7] includes the following under the title "The Order of the Liturgy Service of Palm Sunday":

> They say Alleluia ⲫⲁⲓ ⲡⲉ ⲡⲓ`ⲉϩⲟⲟⲩ as usual, followed by the Readings until the Praxis. Then, they chant the full Hosanna Hymn, which is... etc[8].

> They say Agios three times, then read the Psalm after the Litany of the Gospel[9], and respond with two words in the

---

[7] The same also came in the *Manuscript of Al-Baramūs Monastery 1514*. Refer to: Samuel of Shibīn Al-Qanater, *op. cit.*, 61.
[8] The manuscript includes the hymn in Coptic. I have previously included the full text of the hymn in its original language, Greek.
[9] The Church Order manuscript did not include the first few words of the Psalm Reading as it did before the fourth Gospel

Sinjārī Tune and two words in the Annual Tune. If the patriarch or bishop is present, they say Ⲙⲁⲣⲟⲩϭⲁⲥϥ ... (that is: Let them exalt Him). Then, the former says Ἰⲣⲏⲛⲏ ⲡⲁⲥⲓⲛ ... (that is: Peace be with all), and they respond saying Ⲕⲉ ⲧⲱ Ⲡ̅ⲛ̅ⲁ̅ⲧⲓ ⲥⲟⲩ (that is: And with your spirit). Before the second and third Gospel Reading Ⲙⲁⲣⲟⲩϭⲁⲥϥ... is not said, but only Ἰⲣⲏⲛⲏ ⲡⲁⲥⲓⲛ... and they respond with Ⲕⲉ ⲧⲱ Ⲡ̅ⲛ̅ⲁ̅ⲧⲓ ⲥⲟⲩ. The patriarch or bishop then reads all the Gospel Readings in Coptic. The first is from St. Matthew.[10] After translating it in Arabic, they chant the first hymn of Ὠⲥⲁⲛⲛⲁ (Hosanna). Afterwards, he (the patriarch) reads the second Gospel Reading from St. Mark[11] and they interpret it and respond with the second Hosanna Hymn. Then, he (the patriarch) reads the third Gospel Reading from St. Luke[12] and they interpret and respond with the third Hosanna Hymn.

Then, they read the Psalm Versicle of Ἰⲛⲉⲟⲕ Ⲫϯ ʾϥⲉⲣϣⲁⲩ ⲛⲁⲕ ... (that is: Praise is awaiting You, O God) and respond either with the short Sinjārī or the usual Annual Tune. If the patriarch was present, they say Ⲙⲁⲣⲟⲩϭⲁⲥϥ ... and read the fourth Gospel from St. John,[13] which is then interpreted by the serving deacon. They say the response,[14] followed by ʾⲰⲥⲁⲩⲧⲱⲥ.... If the patriarch was not present, the priests or the deacons read the three Gospel Readings and respond as

---

Reading. It is the Psalm that starts with ⲁⲣⲓⲥⲁⲗⲡⲓⲍⲓⲛ ϧⲉⲛ ⲟⲩⲥⲟⲩⲁⲓ "Blow the trumpet at the time of the New Moon..." (Psalm 80:3, 1, 2).
[10] Matthew 21:1-17
[11] Mark 11:1-11
[12] Luke 19:29-48
[13] John 12:12-19
[14] I will include this response later, which starts with: "He who sits upon the Cherubim rode on a donkey and entered Jerusalem."

previously explained. Then, they chant the Psalm, and the service deacon reads the fourth Gospel and translates it into Arabic. They respond as follows:

He who sits upon the Cherubim, rode on a donkey, and entered Jerusalem, oh what this great humility.	Ⲫⲏⲉⲧϩⲉⲙⲥⲓ ϩⲓϫⲉⲛ ⲛⲓⲭⲉⲣⲟⲩⲃⲓⲙ : ⲁϥⲧⲁⲗⲏⲟⲩⲧ ʽⲉⲟⲩʽⲉʽⲱ : ⲁϥϣⲉ ʽ ⲉⲃⲟⲩⲛ ʽⲉⲓⲗⲏⲙ : ⲟⲩⲡⲉ ⲡⲁⲓⲛⲓⲱϯ ʽ ⲛⲑⲉⲃⲓʽⲟ.[15]

They continue as usual, and the priest starts the Liturgy. The Aspasmos reads:

Christ our Saviour, in great humility, entered Jerusalem, riding on a donkey. The young children, praise Emmanuel saying, "Hosanna in the highest, this is the King of Israel."	Ⲡⲭ̅ⲥ̅ Ⲡⲉⲛⲥⲱ̅ⲣ̅ : ϧⲉⲛ ⲟⲩⲛⲓⲱϯ ʽⲛⲑⲉⲃⲓⲟ : ⲁϥϣⲉ ʽⲉⲃⲟⲩⲛ ʽⲉⲓⲗⲏⲙ : ⲉϥⲧⲁⲗⲏⲟⲩⲧ ʽⲉⲟⲩʽⲉʽⲱ . Ⲛⲓⲕⲟⲩϫⲓ ʽⲛʽⲁⲗⲱⲟⲩʽⲓ : ⲉⲩϩⲱⲥ ϫⲉ Ⲉⲙⲙⲁⲛⲟⲩⲏⲗ : ʽⲱⲥⲁⲛⲛⲁ ϧⲉⲛ ⲛⲏⲉⲧϭⲟⲥⲓ : ⲫⲁⲓ ⲡⲉ ʽⲡⲟⲩⲣⲟ ʽⲙⲡⲓⲥ̅ⲗ̅ .
That we may praise…	Ϩⲓⲛⲁ ʽⲛⲧⲉⲛ … …

Then, they continue the Liturgy. At the time of distributing the Holy Sacraments, then say ⲁ̅ⲗ̅ ʽⲥⲙⲟⲩ ʽⲉⲫϯ, followed by Ϫⲉ ʽϥʽⲥⲙⲁⲣⲱⲟⲩⲧ … in the Tune of the Cross.

4. The Manuscripts under Study

---

[15] The *Church Order Manuscript No. 118 (Rites) in Cairo Patriarchate for the year 1911* includes the full text in Coptic only as usual.

The *Manuscript of the Roman Quarter Typikon (15th century)* mentions the following:

After the Praxis they chant the Hymn of the Feast followed by Agios[16] three times and the following verses in the likes of ˋⲪⲚⲀⲨ ˋⲘⲠⲒˋⲤⲘⲞⲨ:

He who sits upon the Cherubim, rode on a donkey, and entered Jerusalem, oh what this great humility.	ⲪⲎⲈⲦϨⲈⲘⲤⲒ ϨⲒϪⲈⲚ ⲚⲒⲬⲈⲢⲞⲨⲂⲒⲘ : ⲈϤⲦⲀⲖⲎⲞⲨⲦ ˋⲈⲞⲨˋⲈˋⲰ : ⲀϤϢⲈ ˋ ⲈϦⲞⲨⲚ ˋⲈⲒⲖⲎⲘ : ⲞⲨⲠⲈ ⲠⲀⲒⲚⲒⲰϯ ˋ ⲚⲐⲈⲂⲒˋⲞ.[17]
Then He completed the saying of David the spirit-bearer, who likewise said, "Out of the mouths of babes and nursing infants You have perfected praise[18].	ⲦⲞⲦⲈ ⲀϤϪⲰⲔ ˋⲈⲂⲞⲖ ˋⲘⲠⲒⲤⲀϪⲒ : ˋⲚⲦⲈ ⲆⲀⲨⲒⲆ ⲠⲒˋⲠⲚⲈⲨⲘⲀⲦⲞⲪⲞⲢⲞⲤ : ϪⲈ ˋ ⲈⲂⲞⲖϦⲈⲚ ⲢⲰⲞⲨ ˋⲚϨⲀⲚⲔⲞⲨϪⲒ : ˋⲚˋ ⲀⲖⲰⲞⲨˋⲒ ⲀⲔⲤⲈⲂⲦⲈ ⲠⲒˋⲤⲘⲞⲨ.
They praise Him watchfully, saying: 'This is Emmanuel, hosanna in the highest, this is the King of Israel[19]'.	ⲤⲈϨⲰⲤ ˋⲈⲢⲞϤ ϦⲈⲚ ⲞⲨⲚⲈϨⲤⲒ : ⲀⲨϪⲈ ⲪⲀⲒ ⲠⲈ ⲈⲘⲘⲀⲚⲞⲨⲎⲖ : ˋⲰⲤⲀⲚⲚⲀ ϦⲈⲚ ⲚⲎⲈⲦϬⲞⲤⲒ : ⲪⲀⲒ ⲠⲈ ˋⲠⲞⲨⲢⲞ ˋⲘⲠⲒˋ ⲤⲢⲀⲎⲖ.

---

[16] The manuscript only includes two verses.
[17] The manuscript includes the Coptic text only.
[18] This verse neither appeared in the Church Order manuscript nor in the book of *The Typikon and Order of the Passion Week and the Glorious Passover Feast (1920)*. Therefore, I include the full text here in accordance with the *Manuscript of the Roman Quarter Typikon (15th century)* for when the other references include the verse that directly follows, ignoring this one, the meaning does not flow naturally.
[19] *The Typikon and Order of the Passion Week and the Glorious Passover Feast (1920)* includes a verse following this one, which reads: "Let

| The cherubim worship Him… | Ⲛⲓⲭⲉⲣⲟⲩⲃⲓⲙ ⲥⲉⲟⲩⲱϣⲧ `ⲙⲙⲟϥ …²⁰ |

Then they say the Litany of the Gospel and the Psalm and they respond in the Sinjārī tune. The first Gospel is from St. Matthew, and then the congregation chants the following from the hymn of the feast

| Hosanna in the highest, and again in the highest. | Ⲱⲥⲁⲛⲛⲁ ⲉⲛ ⲧⲓⲥ `ⲩⲯⲓⲥⲧⲓⲥ : ⲡⲁⲗⲓⲛ ⲉⲛ ⲧⲓⲥ `ⲩⲯⲓⲥⲧⲏⲥ |

Afterwards, they read the second Gospel from St. Mark, starting with Ⲕⲁⲧⲁ Ⲙⲁⲣⲕⲟⲛ `ⲁⲅⲓⲟⲩ.²¹ It starts²² in Arabic with 'A reading from the Gospel of St. Mark the Evangelist'. After translating the second Gospel, they respond with the hymn of the feast, saying

| Hosanna to the Son of David, and again to the Son of David. | Ⲱⲥⲁⲛⲛⲁ ⲧⲱ `ⲩⲓⲱ Ⲇⲁⲩⲓⲇ : ⲡⲁⲗⲓⲛ ⲧⲱ `ⲩⲓⲱ Ⲇⲁⲩⲓⲇ |

---

us say with David the psalmist, 'Blessed is He who comes in the name of the Lord, the Good One from now and unto the end of ages.'"

[20] I think that this verse was incorrectly copied, for it is supposed to be: Ⲛⲓⲭⲉⲣⲟⲩⲃⲓⲙ ⲛⲉⲙ ⲛⲓⲥⲉⲣⲁⲫⲓⲙ: ⲛⲓⲁⲅⲅⲉⲗⲟⲥ ⲛⲉⲙ ⲛⲓⲁⲣⲭⲏⲁⲅⲅⲉⲗⲟⲥ …, that is "The cherubim, the seraphim, the angels and the archangels…" This is the verse that is constantly repeated in all Lordly feasts, along with the one that follows it, which includes the Praise of the Angles: "Glory be to God in the highest…" The latter glorification is a core liturgical component in all the different Lordly feasts.

[21] That is: "according to St. Mark."

[22] Written differently in the Arabic text.

Then they read the third Gospel from St. Luke, starting with Ⲕⲁⲧⲁ ⲗⲟⲩⲕⲁⲛ. It starts in Arabic with 'A reading from the Gospel of St. Luke the Evangelist'. After the third Gospel, they respond with the hymn of the feast: ⲁ̅ⲗ̅ ⲁ̅ⲗ̅ ⲕⲉ ⲁ̅ⲗ̅ ⲡⲁⲗⲓⲛ ⲕⲉ ⲁ̅ⲗ̅.[23]

Afterwards, they read this Psalm on the fourth Gospel ˋⲚⲑⲟⲕ Ⲫ̇ⲧ ˋⲉⲣⲱⲁⲩ ⲛⲁⲕ ...,[24] and circle around the sanctuary with the Bible. The reader then ascends to the pulpit and reads the fourth Gospel from St. John, starting with Ⲉⲩⲗⲟⲅⲏⲥⲟⲛ ⲉⲕ ⲧⲟⲩ ⲕⲁⲧⲁ Ⲓⲱ̅ⲁ̅. It begins in Arabic with the usual 'Stand up[25] in the fear of God and listen to the Holy Gospel'.

After reading the fourth Gospel in Arabic, they chant the Gospel Response in the Hosanna Tune

| And at the time Christ rode on a donkey in humility, the children praised Him saying: Hosanna in the highest. | Ⲟⲩⲟϩ ϧⲉⲛ ˋⲫⲛⲁⲩ ⲉϥⲧⲁⲗⲏⲟⲩⲧ ˋⲉⲟⲩⲉⲱ ˋⲛⲝⲉ Ⲡ̅ⲭ̅ⲥ̅ ϧⲉⲛ ⲟⲩⲑⲉⲃⲓ ˋⲟ ⲛⲓⲁⲗⲱⲟⲩ ˋⲓ ⲉⲩϩⲱⲥ ˋⲉⲣⲟϥ ϫⲉ ⲱⲥⲁⲛⲛⲁ ϧⲉⲛ ⲛⲏⲉⲧϭⲟⲥⲓ. |

After the second stanza of the Aspasmos, they say – if they were praying the liturgy according to St. Gregory or St. Basil on the day

| Hosanna in the highest. Blessed is He who comes in the name of the Lord. Hosanna in the highest. | Ⲱⲥⲁⲛⲛⲁ ⲉⲛ ⲧⲓⲥ ⲯⲓⲥⲧⲏⲥ ⲉⲩⲗⲟⲅⲏⲙⲉⲛⲟⲥ ˋⲟ ⲁⲣⲭⲱⲛ ⲕⲉ |

---

[23] That is: "Alleluia. Alleluia, and Alleluia. And again Alleluia."
[24] The manuscripts include the full text of the Psalm in Coptic.
[25] Written differently in the Arabic text.

> ⲉⲣⲭⲟⲙⲉⲛⲟⲥ ⲉⲛ ⲟⲩⲛⲟⲙⲁⲧⲓ Ⲕⲉ
> ⲱⲥⲁⲛⲛⲁ ⲉⲛ ⲧⲓⲥ ⲯⲓⲥⲧⲏⲥ .

At the end of the service, they recite ⲇⲗ`ⲥⲙⲟⲩ `ⲉ`Ⲫ︦ϯ ϧⲉⲛ ⲛⲏⲉⲑⲟⲩⲁⲃ,[26] and conclude in the Hosanna Tune, saying ϫⲉ `ϥ`ⲥⲙⲁⲣⲱⲟⲩⲧ.[27]

Afterwards, they pray the Funeral Prayer... etc."

The *Manuscript of Abba Shenoute Typikon (15th century)* includes the Rite of the Palm Sunday Liturgy with the following note:

After the Praxis Reading, they chant the Hosanna Hymn, followed by the Trisagion and the Litany of the Gospel.

The four Gospel Responses mentioned in this manuscript are the same as in most other manuscripts under study[28], such that the first Gospel Response is ⲱⲥⲁⲛⲛⲁ ⲧⲱ `ⲩⲓⲱ ⲇⲁⲩⲓⲇ..., the second is ⲱⲥⲁⲛⲛⲁ ⲉⲛ ⲧⲓⲥ `ⲩⲯⲓⲥⲧⲓⲥ..., and the third is ⲱⲥⲁⲛⲛⲁ ⲃⲁⲥⲓⲗⲓ ⲧⲟⲩ Ⲓⲥⲣⲁⲏⲗ ...

The manuscript includes the fourth Gospel Response as follows:

---

[26] This is Psalm 150 "Praise God in all His saints..."
[27] That is: Blessed be the Father and the Son... etc.
[28] Except for the *Manuscript of the Roman Quarter Typikon (15th century)* which includes a different order for the four Gospel Responses.

He who sits upon the Cherubim, rode on a donkey, and entered Jerusalem, oh what this great humility. Christ rode on a donkey, in humility, the children glorified saying, "Hosanna in the highest. This is the King of Israel."[30]	ⲪⲎⲦⲌⲈⲘⲤⲒ ϨⲒⲬⲈⲚ ⲚⲒⲬⲈⲢⲞⲨⲂⲒⲘ : ⲈϤⲦⲀⲖⲎⲞⲨⲦ ʼⲈⲞⲨʼⲈʼⲰ : ⲀϤϢⲈ ʼ ⲈϦⲞⲨⲚ ʼⲈⲒⲎ̅Ⲙ̅ : ⲞⲨⲠⲈ ⲠⲀⲒⲚⲒⲰϯ ʼ ⲚⲐⲈⲂⲒʼⲞ.[29] ⲞⲨⲞϨ ϦⲈⲚ ʼⲪⲚⲀⲨ ⲈϤⲦⲀⲖⲎⲞⲨⲦ ʼ ⲈⲞⲨⲈⲰ ⲈⲨϨⲰⲤ ϨⲀⲬⲰϤ ʼⲚⲬⲈ ⲚⲒⲀⲖⲰⲞⲨʼⲒ ⲬⲈ ⲰⲤⲀⲚⲚⲀ ϦⲈⲚ ⲚⲎⲈⲦϬⲞⲤⲒ ⲪⲀⲒ ⲠⲈ ʼⲠⲞⲨⲢⲞ ʼⲘⲠⲤⲖ.

The *Manuscript of Abba Shenoute Typikon (15th century)* goes on to say:

If the patriarch was present, they say ⲘⲁⲣⲟⲩϬⲁⲥϥ after the Psalm as usual, and he is the one to read the Gospels, one by one while they respond as previously mentioned. Then, they recite the fourth Psalm and Gospel and respond as previously noted. After the aforementioned response they say this verse to honour the patriarch ʼⲰⲤⲀⲨⲦⲞⲤ ⲦⲈⲚϬⲒⲤⲒ ʼ

---

[29] The manuscript includes the Coptic text only.
[30] This second verse is similar to the one that came as a response to the fourth Gospel in the *Manuscript of the Roman Quarter Typikon (15th century)*, while the *Manuscript of the Hanging Church Typikon (16th century)* mentions that, after the fourth Gospel Reading, they respond with the first verse mentioned in the text. The aforementioned manuscript then states: "And after that this verse. Then, whosoever reads this verse specifically on its own. The judgment is left to the reader." Then it includes this second verse mention in the text. The *Manuscript of London Typikon* includes these two verses together as a response to the fourth Gospel. Do not forget, dear reader, that the *Church Order Manuscript No. 118 (Rites) in Cairo Patriarchate for the year 1911* includes the first verse only as a response to the fourth Gospel.

ⲙⲙⲟⲕ, and then continue the Liturgy Service. When they reach the Reconciliation Prayer, they say this verse first - 'Behold the young children praise Emmanuel saying: Hosanna in the highest, this is the King of Israel'[31] and then continue as usual.

The rest of the Liturgy Service is carried out[32] in the annual rite until the end, which is the custom of the Hanging Church and appropriate to the occasion. However, it is customary in some churches to begin the Funeral Prayer immediately following the Liturgy Service, which is inappropriate. This morning is a Lordly feast, and the oblations are worthy of all honour and reverence. Thus, in the Hanging Church, they start[33] reading Psalm 150 ⲁⲗ ` ⲥⲙⲟⲩ `ⲉⲫϯ without hymn until the end, followed by one verse in the Tune of the Cross - ⲭⲉ `ⲕ`ⲥⲙⲁⲣⲱⲟⲩⲧ. They end the Service in joy and gladness in honour of the Holy Body. Afterwards, they begin reciting the Funeral Prayer, beginning with the Coptic Epistle and its introduction... etc.

The *Manuscript of Haret Zuweila Typikon (17th century)*[34] includes the following:

---

[31] The manuscript includes the text in both Coptic and Arabic. The same verse is mention in *The Guide and Order of the Passion Week and the Glorious Passover Feast* (1920) but preceded by another verse: our Saviour, in great humility, entered Jerusalem, riding on a donkey.
[32] Written differently in the Arabic text.
[33] Written differently in the Arabic text.
[34] The same is mentioned in the *Manuscript of the Hanging Church Typikon (16th century)*.

... At the end of reading the Praxis in Arabic, they say the Hosanna Hymn Ⲉⲩⲗⲟⲅⲏⲙⲉⲛⲟⲥ, followed by the Trisagion and afterwards they say

He who sits upon the Cherubim, rode on a donkey, and entered Jerusalem, oh what this great humility.	Ⲫⲏⲉⲧϩⲉⲙⲥⲓ ϩⲓⲭⲉⲛ Ⲛⲓⲭⲉⲣⲟⲩⲃⲓⲙ: ⲉϥⲧⲁⲗⲏⲟⲩⲧ ʽⲉⲟⲩʽⲉʽⲱ: ⲁϥϣⲉ ʽ ⲉⲃⲟⲩⲛ ʽⲉⲓⲗⲏⲙ: ⲟⲩⲡⲉ ⲡⲁⲓⲛⲓϣϯ ʽ ⲛⲑⲉⲃⲓʽⲟ.³⁵
The cherubim...	Ⲛⲓⲭⲉⲣⲟⲩⲃⲓⲙ ...

Then, they pray the Litany of the Gospel... and continue the Liturgy until the end as usual. They pray the usual Psalm 150 ⲁⲗ ʽⲥⲙⲟⲩ ʽⲉʽⲫϯ and Ⳉⲉ ʽϥʽⲥⲙⲁⲣⲱⲟⲩⲧ without hymn. They say one verse in the tune of the feast, then begin reciting the Funeral Prayer, which begins with the introduction to the Pauline as follows... They pray the Funeral Prayer in order as previously explicated until the end of Communion. In some churches, they do not pray ⲁⲗ ʽⲥⲙⲟⲩ ʽⲉʽⲫϯ or Ⳉⲉ ʽϥʽⲥⲙⲁⲣⲱⲟⲩⲧ but begin the Funeral Prayer immediately following the Liturgy. However, this practice is inappropriate as it disregards the sacrifice. The rite of the sacrifice should be completed as previously detailed, for this is appropriate and right... etc.

The *Manuscript of London Typikon* includes the same order for the Hosanna Liturgy Service as in most other manuscripts.[36] After the Praxis they say the

---

[35] The manuscript includes the Coptic text only.
[36] Except for the *Manuscript of the Roman Quarter Typikon (15th century)* which includes an important unique liturgical element that is not mentioned in the other manuscripts under study.

Hosanna Hymn, followed by the Trisagion and the Litany of the Gospel.

At the end of the manuscripts' account of the order of the Hosanna Liturgy Service, it reads:

> They continue the Liturgy as usual, then say Alleluia, followed by `ⲥⲙⲟⲩ `ⲉ`ⲫϯ without hymn and Ϫⲉ `ϥ` ⲥⲙⲁⲣⲱⲟⲩⲧ in the Tune of the Cross. This is to honour the Holy Body; thus, the service is concluded in joy and gladness. Afterwards, they begin reciting the Funeral Prayer, which begins with the Pauline... etc.

Second: Commentary on the Order of the Palm Sunday Liturgy Service

The Typikon and Order of the Passion Week and the Glorious Passover Feast (1920) includes an initial rite for the Palm Sunday Liturgy Service that was not mentioned in any of the other old references, not even in the Church Order manuscripts. It reads in p. 83:

> At the time of the Liturgy, the pope dons the liturgical vestment[37] as usual, while the priests take up censers in their hands and the deacons carry candles, Gospels, and palm and olive branches, and go forth to celebrate the patriarch's entry into the church. They chant before him, saying: "Hosanna to the Son of David" until they reach the sanctuary, where they start reciting the Psalms as usual.

---

[37] Written differently in the Arabic text.

The dear reader may be wondering why the Church Order manuscripts did not include this introductory rite. The answer lies in the fact that this introduction is an inadequate addition by the Typikon's authors, for the contradiction it introduces proves that it could not have been derived from any old liturgical references which fully observe the tradition.

When the Typikon says: "the pope dons the liturgical vestments as usual" and then shortly after says: "... to celebrate the entry of the patriarch into the church," it presents a clear contradiction, for, in accordance with the customary tradition that remained until the twentieth century, the pope or bishop wore their liturgical vestments after the offertory and the thanksgiving prayer, and before reading the Absolution of the Servants. Thus, the pope or the bishop wears their vestments when they are already inside the sanctuary and not before entering it, for the priestly vestment, which is appurtenant to the service of the altar, should be worn by the same. The Church ritual still abides by this tradition to this day, which is apparent from the content of the hymns that are chanted at this point of the service in the presence of the officiating pope or bishop.[38]

---

[38] The dear reader may need to refer to my book, *Divine Liturgy: The Mystery of the Kingdom of God*, for further clarification on this matter.

The reason the older liturgical references, as well as the Church Order manuscripts, were silent on this matter lies in the fact that these references already mention that the pope enters the church in a ceremonial procession before the start of the Vespers Praise of Palm Sunday. The pope or the bishop participates in the Vespers Praise of Palm Sunday as previously mentioned in the Typikon.

Therefore, the pope or bishop will also be present from the beginning of the Midnight Praise and the Matins Raising of Incense. The Church history records examples of this, like the participation of Pope Athanasius the Apostolic with the congregation in the midnight vigil of praise that preceded the Sunday Liturgy.[39]

Hence, in accordance with the ancient tradition, the pope or the bishop would be already present in the

---

It is also peculiar that the Typikon mentions that after the thanksgiving prayer they say Cⲱⲉhc, and not Niⲥⲁⲃⲉⲩ ⲧⲏⲣⲟⲩ.

[39] It is an old tradition in the Church of Jerusalem since the fourth century that the pope or the bishop does not attend Vespers or Midnight Praise, and thus enters the church later for special circumstances that were specific to this Church only. However, when this custom propagated to other Churches, it gave an impression among the congregation that these liturgical components of the prayers are not very important but are rather specific to the cantors and some deacons and are prayed in the absence of the priestly orders.

church when the Palm Sunday Liturgy Service begins. However, it seems that by the Middle Ages the pope only entered the church before the beginning of the Matins Raising of Incense prayers, wearing a green vestment, which is different from the priestly garment that he would wear during the Divine Liturgy. In the thirteenth century, Ibn Sebā' says the following on this matter:

> ... in the evening of Lazarus Saturday, they cut palms and olive branches and weave them into one big honourable and glorious olive branch, adorned with crosses and candles, and carry it to the patriarch's cell. In the morning of the Sunday, that is Palm Sunday, the patriarch puts on a green vestment, and they pray as is customary.[40]

During the Middle Ages, since the beginning of the thirteenth century and afterwards, the pope or the bishop would enter the church at the beginning of the Matins Raising of Incense prayers. A few centuries ago, the pope or the bishop proceeded to enter the church at the start of the Divine Liturgy prayers as mentioned in *The Typikon and Order of the Passion Week and the Glorious Passover Feast (1920)*.

I think that the confusion the authors of the Typikon fell into was dealt with by Ibn Sebā' in the thirteenth century when he said:

---

[40] Yoḥanna Ibn Zakaria Ibn Sebā', *op. cit.*, 318.

> At the time of the Divine Liturgy, the patriarch dons the liturgical vestment as usual, while the priests and deacons ascend[41] carrying candles and Gospels. As the patriarch stands before the sanctuary, they carry the olive branch and chant before it chants relevant to this feast. When they descend[42] with the olive branch, the patriarch goes out to meet it at the central door, uncovers his head and places incense in the censer. The attending priests participate with him in their rites. Afterwards, he carries it to the sanctuary and places it by the altar door.[43]

When Ibn Sebā' says: "the patriarch dons the priestly vestment as usual," he is referring to what he previously mentioned that the high priest puts on the priestly garment after the offertory and thanksgiving prayer. About that, he says:

> When the priest concludes the thanksgiving prayer... if the hight priest was present, he would wear the vestment at that time in the likeness of Aaron, while the chanters sing what befits putting on the priestly garment...[44]

The same is observed until today, for the hymn that is chanted while the pope or the bishop is putting on the priestly garment still preserves this old liturgical rite as mentioned by Ibn Sebā'.

---

[41] That is, ascend to the sanctuary.
[42] That is, descend from the sanctuary.
[43] Yoḥanna Ibn Zakaria Ibn Sebā', *op. cit.*, 318.
[44] *Ibid.*, 186-187.

Thus, what Ibn Sebā' mentions about the priests and the deacons ascending with the candles and the Gospels while carrying the olive branch refers to their entry into the sanctuary.

About the Readings of the Palm Sunday Liturgy
The Pauline is taken from Hebrews 9:11-28, the Catholic Epistle from 1 Peter 1-11, and the Praxis from Acts 28:11-38. The Pauline illustrates the entry of Christ, the Passover Lamb, into the Holy of Holies, that is Jerusalem, not many times as in the Old Testament, but once and for all, that He might offer Himself to His Father by His own blood. In this manner, He presented Himself as a ransom for us before the Father. Through Christ we were able to approach the Father, as He has offered Himself, with us in Him, before the Father. Through His sacrifice, Christ abolished the sin that reigned over us, and became for us eternal redemption.

Indeed, this is the foundation of our joy in this feast: we anticipate the events because are already living the time of our salvation.

Then, the Catholic Epistle briefly details in depth the lived experience of sharing in Christ's sufferings, saying,

> Therefore, since Christ suffered for us in the flesh, arm yourselves also with the same mind, for he who has suffered in the flesh has ceased from sin.

The Praxis shows St. Paul the Apostle being chain bound and tied up in Jerusalem for the sake of the hope of Israel.

This is a remarkable and fine selection of readings for the occasion we are celebrating during this feast, which is an unceasing nourishment for meditation for those who enjoy tying spiritual themes together. For now, it is sufficient for us to rejoice in knowing that the readings conclude with good tidings for us Gentiles, saying "Therefore let it be known to you that the salvation of God has been sent to the Gentiles, and they will hear it!" Thank God who made us citizens of His household, close to Him, even united with Him, and enjoying His salvation without hindrance from His or our side.

It is important to point out here that the Praxis Response preceding the Praxis is ϣⲁⲣⲉ Ⲫϯ (Chare Evnoti), which is solely chanted during the days of the Holy Great Lent. This response is the standard one chanted throughout all the occasions of the liturgical year.[45] Therefore, all the Church Order manuscripts, as well as the old liturgical references, are silent about the Praxis Response with

---

[45] Refer to the book of the *Divine Liturgy: The Mystery of the Kingdom of God* for an explanation of the reasoning behind this rite.

respect to all the church occasions that they record. The same is found in *The Typikon and Order of the Passion Week and the Glorious Passover Feast (1920)*.

The Hosanna Hymn and What Follows after the Praxis Reading

After reading the Praxis in Arabic, they chant the Hosanna Hymn, followed by the Trisagion, in accordance with the *Church Order Manuscript No. 118 (Rites) in Cairo Patriarchate 1911* and all the manuscripts under study.

The *Manuscript of the Roman Quarter Typikon (15th century)* mentions that, after the Trisagion, they say three verses for the Palm Sunday Feast, while the manuscripts of the Hanging Church Typikon only include the first verse. However, all manuscripts agree that after these verses for Palm Sunday, they say two other verses that are repeated in all the Lordly Feasts.

The Typikon and Order of the Passion Week and the Glorious Passover Feast (1920) is the only reference that records that these verses are said before the Trisagion, rather than after. It also includes a modification and an addition that the reader, who has followed my explanation, cannot miss. The Typikon includes the following verses that are to be chanted with hymn:

- He who sits upon the Cherubim, rode on a donkey and entered Jerusalem; Oh what is this great humility? ...[46]
- They praise Him with watchfulness saying, "This is Emmanuel, hosanna in the highest, this is the King of Israel."
- Let us say with David the psalmist, "Blessed is He who comes, in the name of the good Lord, from now and until the end of times."[47]
- The Cherubim and the Seraphim, the angels and the archangels, the principalities and the authorities, the thrones and the powers.
- Proclaim saying, "Glory to God in the highest, peace on earth, and goodwill toward men."

These verses that precede the Trisagion, according to the Typikon, were not mentioned in the *Church Order Manuscript No. 118 (Rites) in Cairo Patriarchate 1911*. This latter manuscript, along with the other Church Order manuscripts include verses that are chanted after the Trisagion, instead of before, in feasts other than Palm Sunday.

Chanting these verses after the trisagion is an ancient tradition in all churches. The Typikon is the first to place them before the Trisagion. Regardless of whether they are said before or after there is no overlap between them

---

[46] As mentioned before, the *Manuscript of the Roman Quarter Typikon (15th century)* includes another verse here that connects the meaning of the verses before and after it.
[47] This verse is only mentioned in the Typikon but is not included in the manuscripts.

and the Trisagion as is practiced in some churches today.[48]

The Old Rite of Chanting the Psalms and the Gospels of the Palm Sunday Liturgy

The *Church Order Manuscript No. 118 (Rites) in Cairo Patriarchate 1911* records the rite of chanting the Psalms and the Gospels of the Palm Sunday Liturgy which are mentioned at the beginning of this chapter.

A summary of what the manuscript mentions is as follows:

(a) In case the patriarch or bishop is present in the service:
- The Litany of the Gospel is recited,
- The Psalm is chanted, half in the Sinjārī Tune and the other half in the Annual Tune,
- They say, "Let them exalt Him in the church of His people...,"
- The pope says: Peace be with all,
- The congregation responds: And with your spirit,
- The pope reads the First Gospel from St. Matthew in Coptic,
- The First Gospel from St. Matthew is interpreted in Arabic,
- "Hosanna to the Son of David, again to the Son of David" is chanted with hymn[49],

---

[48] I explain this matter in detail in the book of *The Fast of Nineveh and the Great Holy Lent* for your reference.
[49] That is, the tune of the Hymn of Evlogimenos.

- The pope says: Peace be with all,
- The congregation responds: And with your spirit,
- The pope reads the Second Gospel from St. Mark in Coptic,
- The Second Gospel from St. Mark is interpreted in Arabic,
- "Hosanna in the highest, again in the highest" is chanted with hymn[50],
- The pope says: Peace be with all,
- The congregation responds: And with your spirit,
- The pope reads the Third Gospel from St. Luke in Coptic,
- The Third Gospel from St. Luke is interpreted in Arabic,
- "Hosanna to the King of Israel, again to the King of Israel" is chanted with hymn[51],
- The Psalm, "Praise is awaiting You, O God, in Zion; And to You shall the vow be performed in Jerusalem…" (Psalm 64:1-2), is chanted in the short Sinjārī Tune or the Annual Tune.
- They say, "Let them exalt Him in the church of His people…,"
- The pope says: Peace be with all,
- The congregation responds: And with your spirit,
- The pope reads the Fourth Gospel from St. John in Coptic,
- The Fourth Gospel from St. John is interpreted in Arabic,
- "Hosanna to the Son of David, again to the Son of David" is chanted with hymn,
- The Gospel Response is said:

---

[50] *Ibid.*
[51] The same previous footnote

He who sits upon the Cherubim, rode on a donkey, and entered Jerusalem, oh what this great humility.	ⲫⲏⲉⲧϩⲉⲙⲥⲓ ϩⲓⲭⲉⲛ ⲛⲓⲭⲉⲣⲟⲩⲃⲓⲙ: ⲉϥⲧⲁⲗⲏⲟⲩⲧ ` ⲉⲟⲩ`ⲉ`ⲱ: ⲁϥⲱⲉ `ⲉⲃⲟⲩⲛ ` ⲉⲓⲗⲏⲙ: ⲟⲩⲡⲉ ⲡⲁⲓⲛⲓⲱϯ ` ⲛⲑⲉⲃⲓ`ⲟ.⁵²

- they say: "Likewise we exalt You with David…"

(b) In the case that the patriarch or bishop is not present in the service:
- the priests or the deacons read the three Gospels and respond as previously indicated,
- the Gospel Psalm is chanted,
- the serving deacon reads the Fourth Gospel from St. John,
- the Fourth Gospel Response as indicated is chanted.

The abovementioned is the rite that prevailed in the Church since the Middle Ages until the beginning of the twentieth century – as evinced by the Church Order manuscripts when *The Typikon and Order of the Passion Week and the Glorious Passover Feast (1920)* was published. The latter has omitted from the rite the piece where the patriarch says "Peace be with all" and the congregation responds "And with your spirit" before the Gospel Reading in Coptic. I do not understand with what authority anyone could add or remove what they fancy from the rituals of the prayers, especially under

---

[52] The *Church Order Manuscript No. 118 (Rites) in Cairo Patriarchate 1911* includes the Coptic text only as usual.

the title of a Coptic Prayer Book that reads: "... in accordance with the tradition and rite of the Coptic Orthodox Church"!

We cannot say that the reason for this exclusion is that the pope or the bishop no longer reads the four Gospels in Coptic, for the same Typikon mentions that: "these four Gospels are read in Coptic by the pope, or by the senior priest if the pope, the metropolitan or bishop is not present."

Even if the pope or the bishop read the Fourth Gospel in Coptic only, or if all the Gospels were read in Arabic only, we ought not simply abolish an original ancient rite that prevailed in the Church for many centuries.[53]

One of the many recent editions of the book "The Service of the Deacon and the Hymns"[54] seems to have removed

---

[53] In fact, we lack the certainty that anyone whatsoever has the right to remove or add whatever they like in our copies of ancient books and manuscripts which describe the church rituals and texts of prayer. And if they were compelled to do so for whatever reason, they ought to explain in writing what they have added or omitted. With all gratitude, I would like to mention the good example of what Fr Abd El-Messeh Saleeb El-Baramosy (1848-1935) did in recording the footnotes that came in the Book of the Holy Euchologion which was published in 1902. If it were not for these precise footnotes, many of the rituals of the Divine Liturgy would have been totally forgotten, and the old rites would have been mixed up with the new.

[54] Published by the Central Coptic Orthodox Church Renaissance Association in Cairo.

the responses for the four Gospels and replaced them with other responses. And instead of responding with pleading cries, saying: "Hosanna to the Son of David," "Hosanna in the highest," "Hosanna to the King of Israel," we now recite some poetic verses from Arabic odes that are repeated in Vespers and Matins of Palm Sunday, which are relayed in mere descriptive fashion:
- He who sits upon the Cherubim, today appeared in Jerusalem, riding on a colt with great glory, surrounded by ranks of angels.
- On the way they spread garments, and from the trees they cut branches, while proclaiming with hymns, "Hosanna to the Son of David."
- Today the sayings are fulfilled, from the prophecies and proverbs, as Zechariah prophesied and said, a prophecy about Jesus Christ.

The ritual of reading four Gospels about Christ's entry into the holy city of Jerusalem in the Liturgy Service of Palm Sunday is unique to the Coptic Church and unknown by other churches. The same ritual is repeated in the Gospels of the Eve and Morning of Good Friday of the Holy Pascha.

The Lectionary of Gospel Readings (L'évangéliaire) in the Leyden Church in Holland also mentions four Gospel Readings, but it does not require the reader to read all of them. In fact, Ibn Kabar (1324) did not specify which Gospels are to be read on Palm Sunday. Rather, it appears that in the Liturgy Service he illustrates on this day only one Gospel was read, while the other Gospels that were not mentioned were read at the various stops of the Hosanna Procession that highlights the rite of this day.[55]

An Overview of the Palm Sunday Liturgy Service in Macarius Monastery in the mid-Fourteenth Century
We have documentary evidence on the Palm Sunday Liturgy Service in the mid-fourteenth century in St. Macarius Monastery at the time of Pope Peter V (1340-1348), the 83rd Patriarch, when he made the Holy Chrism at that monastery in the year 1340 AD. We read the following in *Manuscript No. 100 (Arabic)*, currently kept at the National Library of Paris:

> Then they started the Third and Sixth Hour prayers, followed by the Liturgy. The patriarch officiated the Liturgy, assisted by Fr Anba Georgy surnamed Anba Daniel. The pope changed[56], as did the rest of the attending bishops and priests from the monastery. Anba Abram, Bishop of Al-Qusiya, read the epistle[57], which was then translated by Anba Mark, Bishop of Al- Behera. The archdeacon of the holy monastery read the Catholic Epistle, while Anba Gabriel, Bishop of Taha, read the Praxis, which was then translated by Anba Jacob, Bishop of Abou Tij. Then, they chanted the Psalm in the Sinjārī Tune. The First Gospel was read by Anba Tadros, Bishop of Bessat, the

---

[55] Dom Emmanuel Lanne, *op. cit.*, 286-287.
[56] That is, put on the service garment.
[57] That is, the Pauline Reading in Coptic.

Second Gospel by Anba Gabriel, Bishop of Tandata[58], the Third Gospel by Anba Peter, Bishop of Al-Queis, and the Fourth Gospel by the pope, which was then interpreted by Anba Georgy. Then they resumed the Liturgy Service as usual.

At the time of distributing the Holy Sacrament the monks recited the Funeral Prayer. Due to the large crowd gathered on this day, they finished the entire Funeral Prayer by the time the Holy Sacrament was distributed to all the congregation. Afterwards, Bishop Anba Peter read the Litany of the Departed, then the patriarch said the Absolution, and the congregation was dismissed glorifying the Son of God.[59]

The Conclusion Prayer of the Palm Sunday Divine Liturgy

Ibn Sebā'

Afterwards, the patriarch, along with the priests, ascends to the sanctuary and continues the Liturgy of St. Gregory as customary. Then, he dismisses the congregation to eat, reminding them to attend the Funeral Prayer at the Ninth Hour.

Ibn Sebā' confirms this matter once again when he illustrates the Funeral Prayers in Chapter 100 of his book, *The Precious Jewel in Church Sciences (Ketāb al-*

---

[58] Which is currently the city of Tanta.
[59] *Manuscript No. 100 (Arabic)* at the National Library of Paris.

Jawhara al-Nafisa fi 'Oloum al-Kanīsa), under the title "The Funeral of the Living at the Ninth Hour of Palm Sunday outside of the Liturgy."

He says:

> After the Ninth Hour of Palm Sunday, all the Christian people: men and women, servants and maidens, young and infants, gather in church to attend the General Funeral Prayer.[60]

Ibn Kabar

The *Manuscript of Paris* and the *Manuscript of Uppsala* state the following:

> ... And when the Liturgy is over[61] and they have started Holy Communion, they do not chant Psalm 150, but rather recite the Funeral Prayer, one reading after the other, from the Pauline Epistle, the Psalm and Gospel[62] which are specific to the departed until they finish the Communion to occupy the congregation with readings until the end of the distribution.

Commentary and Interpretation

According to Ibn Sebā', the congregation is dismissed after the Divine Liturgy on Palm Sunday, and then

---

[60] Yoḥanna Ibn Zakaria Ibn Sebā', *op. cit.*, 322.
[61] *Manuscript of Uppsala*: is finished.
[62] *Manuscript of Uppsala*: and the Gospels.

return to church around three o'clock in the afternoon to attend the prayers of the General Funeral.

Thus, it is obvious here that, until the thirteenth or fourteenth century, at least some churches in Egypt used to conduct the General Funeral prayers separate from the Palm Sunday Liturgy, while other churches began the General Funeral prayers during the distribution, as was practiced in the mid-fourteenth century in St. Macarius' monastery for example. The latter can also be found in Ibn Kabar (1324), who indicates that in his time the Funeral Prayers were held right after the Palm Sunday Liturgy.

However, what is mentioned by Ibn Kabar here is a circumstance that arose over the original ritual which used to separate the time of the Distribution of the Mysteries from the General Funeral prayers. This is mentioned in *The Typikon and Order of the Passion Week and the Glorious Passover Feast (1920)*, which reads (p. 86):

> They continue the Liturgy until the end, and chant Psalm 150 ` ̀Cмоү `ⲉⲫϯ, followed by one verse in the Hosanna Tune of Ϫⲉ `ϥ`ⲥⲙⲁⲣⲱⲟⲩⲧ and the Funeral Prayer.

What the Typikon mentions seems to indicate that the Funeral Prayer is held during the Distribution of the Mysteries. However, most of the manuscripts under study say otherwise, as we have previously seen in the

Manuscript of Abba Shenoute Typikon (14th century), the *Manuscript of the Hanging Church Typikon (16th century)*, the *Manuscript of Haret Zuweila Typikon (17th century)*, and the *Manuscript of the Hanging Church*.

Hence, we find ourselves with two ritual practices, the first separating the prayers of the Divine Liturgy from the General Funeral, and the second joining them together with no time difference.

The growing number of Christians and the overcrowding of churches with worshippers, due to the small number of churches and the growth of awareness of Holy Communion's importance, have helped in propagating the second practice, especially in cathedrals and churches of large cities, as it became increasingly difficult for the entire congregation to return to the church to attend the prayers of the General Funeral. On the other hand, the first practice is better suited for churches in small villages and monasteries before becoming inundated with visitors and worshippers during these occasions.

Being accustomed to the second ritual, that is, joining the prayers of the General Funeral with the end of the Divine Liturgy, should not cause us to forget that the original tradition was to separate the two.

Therefore, would it not be fitting to chant Psalm 150 at the end of the Divine Liturgy, along with responses and hymns that follow until the end of the Distribution of the Mysteries, and then immediately begin the prayers of the General Funeral?

The Divine Liturgy, especially the time of the Distribution of the Sacraments are true moments of eternal life where every sorrow and grief are taken away, and hence exclude any funeral hymns.

The same is explained in the *Church Order Manuscript No. 118 (Rites) in Cairo Patriarchate 1911* which clearly says:

> Then they continue the Liturgy until the time of the Distribution of the Holy Mysteries when they say ⲁⲗ̀ Ⲥⲙⲟⲩ ⲉ̀ⲫϯ, followed by Ϫⲉ ⲯ̀ⲥⲙⲁⲣⲱⲟⲩⲧ... in the Tune of the Cross. Afterwards, they start reading the Funeral Prayer at the pulpit, as ought to be done.

On the other hand, *The Typikon and Order of the Passion Week and the Glorious Passover Feast (1920)* copies from the Church Order manuscripts and the other manuscripts under study, of which some say:

> They continue the Liturgy until the end, and chant Psalm 150 ˋ ˙Ⲥⲙⲟⲩ ˋⲉⲫϯ, followed by one verse in the Hosanna Tune Ϫⲉ ˋⲯ̀ⲥⲙⲁⲣⲱⲟⲩⲧ and the Funeral Prayer...

This last expression, "followed by one verse," was not mentioned in the Church Order manuscripts at hand.

Starting the Funeral Prayer immediately after the end of the Divine Liturgy has caused Psalm 150 to lose its special tune on this day, that is the Hosanna or the Tune of the Cross. As a result, nowadays in the Coptic Church, we do not have a Hosanna tune for "Alleluia" that precedes Psalm 150, while we have special tunes for other church occasions, that is for the annual season, joyful occasions, the month of Koiak and the Holy Great Lent. Furthermore, chanting Psalm 150 quickly and hastily in order to begin the Funeral Prayer has caused us to miss the proper response in between the Psalm verses as is the custom in other Lordly Feasts.

If we postpone reading the Funeral Prayer until after the Distribution of the Mysteries to adhere to what came in the Church Order manuscripts, and most other manuscripts under study, then what do we say about the time of the distribution on Maundy Thursday, on which the Church Order manuscripts coincide with the other manuscripts under study that Psalm 150 is not chanted, but the prayer of the Eleventh Hour of Maundy Thursday of the Holy Pascha?

Maybe this appeared in the manuscripts because the Liturgy of Maundy Thursday used to end around sunset. However, today in which the Liturgy ends around noon or in the early afternoon, is there any issue with postponing the prayers of the Eleventh Hour of Maundy Thursday until returning to church after some rest? The authorization of this rite lies in the hands of the ecclesiastical hierarchy alone.

Prayer:
O Lord, our God, how wonderful has become Your name in all the earth. For the greatness of Your beauty is exalted above the heavens. Out of the mouth of little children and infants You have prepared praise. Prepare also, O Lord, our souls for praising You, chanting to You, blessing You, serving You, worshipping You, glorifying You, giving thanks to You, every day and every hour.[63]

What is Said on this Day in the Greek Church?
In the Greek Church, there is a Hypakoi, Tone 6, which is said on this day:

> First, they sang in praise of Christ our God with branches, but then the ungrateful Jews seized Him and crucified Him on the Cross. But with faith unchanging let us ever honour Him as Benefactor, crying always unto Him: Blessed are You Who comes to call back Adam.

---

[63] Fraction for the Father which is said on Palm Sunday or any other time.

They also say the following Kontakion, Tone 6, on this day:

> In heaven, He is seated upon a throne and on earth He rides upon a foal. O Christ our God, accept the praise of the angels and the hymn of the children who cry out to You: Blessed are You who comes to call back Adam.

The Liturgical History of an Old Custom of Reserving the Eucharist after this Liturgy

We read the following in the book of the *History of the Patriarchs*, which is also known as the *History of the Holy Church* as well as in Pope Christodoulos' biography (1047-1077):

> ... The monks of the Monastery of St. Macarius and the priests of Alexandria used to reserve some of the Eucharist and keep it covered from the Sunday of Olives until Great Wednesday. There was Anba Michael, author of the Synodical letter and bishop of Tinnis, there with him.[64] The patriarch expressed disapproval to them of what they did to the Eucharist and mentioned what could happen to it in the way of decay, spoiling, insects, and other things besides which it is not possible for me to describe. He commanded this practice to be abolished and anathematized anyone who should do continue in it afterwards, in the presence of an assembly of bishops in the Monastery of St. Macarius

---

[64] That is, with Pope Christodoulos.

and in the presence of the vicar of Christ, Bukairah Al-Rashidi, the scribe and possessor of the Cross.

Then the monks revolted against the patriarch, and came to him with the iron keys, and said to him: 'You are no better than the fathers who preceded you'. So, he arose angrily, and departed to his cell, and a great tumult[65] ensued. Then the patriarch retrieved from the library of the Monastery of St. Macarius a homily on this, and Anba Michael, his secretary, read it to the assembly. The Lord Christ aided this father to suppress this custom, and he abolished it until now, and no one after reverted to reserving portions of the Eucharist...[66]

What is quite remarkable in this story is that the monks brazenly spoke to Pope Christodoulos: 'You are no better than the fathers who preceded you'. This indicates that some of the patriarchs preceding Pope Christodoulos (1047-1077) kept this custom, so that when Pope Christodoulos wanted to abolish it 'a great tumult ensued'.

For me, this story continued to carry with it a vague history that I could not decipher at all, for I did not know when this custom began as it was practiced by the priests of Alexandria and the monks of the monastery of

---

[65] That is, disturbance and turmoil.
[66] History of the Patriarchs of the Egyptian Church: Severus Ibn Al-Muqaffa' of Al-Ashmūnīn, *History of the Holy Church*, Volume 2, Part 3, edited by Yassā 'abd Al-Masīḥ, Aziz Soriel 'ateya, and Oswald H.E. KHS-Burmester (Cairo: Publications de la Société d'Archéologie Copte, 1959), 172-173.

St. Macarius. The history remained ambiguous in this regard until I read what Dom Villecourt had published in 1923. This is the letter of Anba Macarius, Bishop of Memphis, in the tenth century about the old liturgy of the Chrism and Baptism,[67] which was taken from Manuscript No. 100 (Arabic) in the National Library of Paris. It is continued in another Manuscript No. 44 (Coptic) in the Library of the Vatican.[68]

Soon, the Lord aided me to acquire an original copy of the Paris Manuscript No. 100 (Arabic), which contains the aforementioned letter of Anba Macarius. It clearly alludes to the custom of reserving the Eucharist after the Palm Sunday Liturgy.

The letter says:

> ... The matter that they read on the second day[69] of the Passover Week, they found written that Anba Michael, the great and first patriarch,[70] the one of many tribulations, was asked concerning this, and he answered and said, that the apostles in their time commanded that the people

---

[67] Dom Louis Villecourt, *Le livre du chrême (ms. Paris arabe 100)*, Le Muséon, t. XLI, 1928, 49-80.

[68] A. van Lantschoot, *Le Ms. Vatic. Copte 44 et le livre de Chrême (ms. Paris arabe 100)*, dan Le Muséon, t. XLV, Cahiers 3-4 (Louvain: 1932), 5-6.

[69] That is, the Monday of the Holy Pascha.

[70] Papacy from 743 till 767 AD.

remain not without the offering in these days.⁷¹ And they commanded that a large portion of the Eucharist, which is consecrated on Palm Sunday, be left on the altar, and they fraction it a Holy Body and sprinkle it with Blood from the chalice that was consecrated that day. It becomes the Body, commingled, prepared for the third day⁷², and they commune the people from it. In my opinion, this offering was made in Alexandria, wherein is the throne, and in the monasteries, which is the place of the saintly fathers, and we must partake of it without doubt.

The book "History of the Patriarchs" says the following about this Pope Michael I:

... Now our father, Anba Michael, was sweet in speech, beautiful in countenance, perfect in stature, decent in his attire, well-formed and dignified; and his words were like a sword against the rebellious, and his teaching was like salt to people of virtue and modesty. And the hand of God was with him... Now his beard had been full and handsome, flowing over his breast like the beard of Jacob Israel... When he discoursed to us, he spoke a spiritual language like the music of a harp, while the breath of life came forth from his mouth with spiritual praises; and he persevered in fasting and in prayer day and night...⁷³

---

[71] The letter did not specify which days it was referring to; so, did it mean the days of the Pascha in general or the Monday, Tuesday, and Wednesday of the Holy Pascha?
[72] That is, the Tuesday of the Holy Pascha.
[73] History of the Patriarchs by Severus Ibn Al-Muqaffa' of Al-Ashmūnīn, Vol. 2, verified by Samuel of Shibīn Al-Qanater, 1999, 164, 175, 178.

Thus, the practice of reserving the Eucharist after the Palm Sunday Liturgy in both Alexandria and the monastery of St. Macarius for communion on the days of the Holy Pascha continued from the time of Pope Michael I (743-767) until Pope Christodoulos (1047-1077) abolished it. That is, it extended over the papacy of twenty patriarchs.

At the time of Pope Michael I, the offering was kept after the Palm Sunday Liturgy for communion on the Tuesday of the Holy Pascha. Does that mean that, on the Tuesday of the Holy Pascha, they used to conduct a presanctified liturgy, which are known in Greek as προηγιασμένη "Progiasmeni,"[74] i.e., elements that were presanctified on Palm Sunday? It seems that this was the practice indeed, as the scholar W.E. Crum mentions in the Manuscript Catalogue, which he published about a Coptic manuscript that is kept in the British Museum under the code (Add. 5997) and dates back to the year 1247 AD and consists of a Lectionary, that following the

---

[74] This is a Byzantine expression meaning "Presanctified Elements." They would hold a short Liturgy over sacrificial gifts that were presanctified in a previous Liturgy. Thus, the Progiasmeni Liturgy does not include all the main components of the Liturgy, especially the sanctification and the invocation. It also includes no readings from the Epistles or the Gospels, except when it is held during the Paschal Week, which is referred to in the Byzantine Church as the "Great Holy Week" and in the Coptic Church as the "Paschal Week."
Refer to my book: Lexicon of Ecclesiastical Terms, Volume 1.

Ninth Hour of Holy Tuesday a celebration of the Liturgy of the Water and Washing Feet preceded a Liturgy.[75]

Dom Emmanuel Lanne argues that this practice was not popular among the people who questioned its legitimacy prompting Pope Michael I to trace it to the time of the Apostles.

Furthermore, Dom Emmanuel Lanne also indicates that Anba Macarius, Bishop of Memphis, has mentioned that, in the tenth century and under the influence of the Syrian rite, the consecration of the Holy Chrism was moved from the sixth Friday of the Great Lent that directly precedes Palm Sunday to Maundy Thursday. This new use was imposed in the third quarter of the tenth century under Pope Ephrem the Syrian (975-978). Perhaps it was at this time that the Rite of Washing Feet was also moved from Holy Tuesday to Maundy Thursday and that the Eucharistic celebration of Holy Tuesday disappeared. This is only a hypothesis that should be confirmed by subsequent research. The Liturgy of the Church of Jerusalem offers us no information on this point.[76]

---

[75] Dom Emmanuel Lanne, *op. cit.*, 288.
[76] Dom Emmanuel Lanne, *op. cit.*, 289.
I have previously mentioned that the custom of reserving the Eucharist after the Palm Sunday Liturgy has continued in the monastery of St. Macarius until the time of Pope Christodoulos (1047-1077).

It is obvious here that we stand before a liturgical dilemma that requires further research and diligent investigation, for the hypothesis that Dom Emmanuel Lanne produces here is rather difficult in that the ritual of the Washing of Feet was transferred from Holy Tuesday to Maundy Thursday and that the Eucharistic celebration that took place on Holy Tuesday disappeared, especially if we separate between the ritual of the Washing of Feet and the Liturgy that followed it. The simpler hypothesis would be that the entire ritual of Holy Tuesday was moved to Maundy Thursday, that is the ritual of the Washing of the Feet as well as the Liturgy that followed it.

What leads me to this hypothesis is the existence of a liturgical unity that binds the Liturgy of the Water with that of the Eucharist on Maundy Thursday. Furthermore, the ritual of the Liturgy on Maundy Thursday is unique and independent from that of any other Liturgy celebrated during the liturgical calendar. I will discuss this in greater detail when we turn to the rite of the Liturgy of Maundy Thursday.

Chapter Six: The Rite of the General Funeral Prayers

Introduction

The General Funeral Prayers that follow the Divine Liturgy on Palm Sunday are a unique rite to the Coptic Church unknown to both Western and Eastern Churches. These are independent prayers that are unrelated to the prayers of the Palm Sunday Divine Liturgy. In fact, according to ancient tradition, they commence after the Distribution of the Mysteries.

The Purpose of the General Funeral Prayer

Its main purpose is to pray over the entire congregation, along with raising incense and the Litany of the Departed, because the Church does not raise incense during Monday, Tuesday, and Wednesday of Holy Pascha. Thus, if any believer should depart on any of these three days, we would have already prayed over them and raised incense in this Funeral Prayer. In such a case, it would be sufficient to bring the deceased to church and read over them the prayers and the final litany in the Funeral Book without raising any incense.

Furthermore, participating willingly in the General Funeral Prayers enables us to briefly and voluntarily taste death, qualifying us to participate in the Lord's passions and death for us, so that we may rejoice in His resurrection in us, and our lives might be from Him, through Him and in Him.

Ibn Sebā'

We have an explanation for these prayers since the thirteenth century, for Ibn Sebā' says the following under the title, 'The Funeral of the Living at the Ninth Hour of Palm Sunday outside of the Liturgy':

> The patriarch, along with the priests, goes up to the sanctuary and continues the Liturgy of St. Gregory as customary. Then, he dismisses the congregation to eat something, reminding them to attend the Funeral Prayer at the Ninth Hour.[1] After the Ninth Hour of Palm Sunday, all the Christian people: men and women, servants and maidens, young and infants,[2] gather in the church to attend the General Funeral.[3] The reason for funeralizing them at this time is that the Passion Week is solely dedicated to the passions and sorrows of Christ, such as the crucifixion and otherwise, and focuses on those who have willingly

---

[1] In one of the editions of *The Precious Jewel in Church Sciences (Ketāb al-Jawhara al-Nafīsa fī 'Oloum al-Kanīsa)*, we read: "and he dismisses the congregation in peace to their homes, glad and rejoicing till the Ninth Hour of the day."
Yoḥanna Ibn Zakaria Ibn Sebā', *op. cit.*, 322.
[2] Given the many times this word has been repeated in the liturgical prayers of this feast, it is important to note that it was written incorrectly in the Arabic text.
[3] Written differently in the Arabic text.

pursued[4] the afflictions.[5] Beside the sorrow of Christ there should be no other sadness. Thus, before embarking on the Week of Christ's Passion, they begin[6] to funeralize[7] the people at this hour so that no funeral would take place to cause[8] sadness, lest another grief shares in that of Christ.[9]

In some versions of the book, *The Precious Jewel in Church Sciences (Ketāb al-Jawhara al-Nafīsa fī 'Oloum al-Kanīsa)*, by Ibn Sebā' we read the following under the title 'About the Funeral of the Living on Palm Sunday':

> ... the reason for funeralizing them at this time is precautionary lest anyone dies during the Paschal Week. No incense should be raised during the Paschal Week except on Thursday and Saturday. Thus, this funeral service covers four days[10] on which funerals and incense should not take place.[11] Instead, if someone should die, they would bring them to the church and pray over them

---

[4] Written differently in the Arabic text.
[5] In some versions of *The Precious Jewel in Church Sciences (Ketāb al-Jawhara al-Nafīsa fī 'Oloum al-Kanīsa)*, it came as "pursued the destruction."
[6] According to the literal text: "they attend to"
[7] According to the literal text: "the federalization of"
[8] According to the literal text: "that results in"
[9] Yoḥanna Ibn Zakaria Ibn Sebā', *op. cit.*, 322-323.
[10] That is, the Monday, Tuesday, Wednesday, and Friday.
[11] This is an incomplete account, because we read the following in Canon No. 11 of Pope Christodoulos (1047-1077): "...During the Great Week there ought to be no absolutions, commemorations or funerals till the end of the Passover Feast." Thus, it is not about raising incense, but the rationale is that there should not be any absolution, commemoration or funeral during the Holy Paschal Week till the conclusion of the prayers of Good Friday.

the relevant funeral pieces without raising incense or the Prayer over the deceased.[12]

Ibn Kabar

The *Manuscript of Paris* and the *Manuscript of Uppsala* state the following:

---

[12] Yoḥanna Ibn Zakaria Ibn Sebā', *op. cit.*, 322.
The same is mentioned in *The Typikon and Order of the Passion Week and the Glorious Passover Feast (1920)* (p. 86), which quotes the book of *The Precious Jewel in Church Sciences (Ketāb al-Jawhara al-Nafisa fi 'Oloum al-Kanīsa)*. However, the former omitted in the beginning of the following sentence that is written in bold: "After the Ninth Hour of Palm Sunday, all the Christian people..." It also deleted in the end the expression "the Prayer Over the Deceased." Then, the Typikon added the following: "The reason we do not celebrate any liturgies during these next three days of Holy Week is because Palm Sunday was the tenth day after the full-moon – the day during which the sheep and the goats were sold for the feast according to the sayings of God in the Torah, "Take unto you a lamb for yourselves without blemish and keep it with you until the fourteenth day, when you shall slaughter it according to the sayings of the Lord. Keep it on the eleventh, the twelfth, and the thirteenth day and slaughter it on the fourteenth day." So, they kept the lamb for three days: Monday, Tuesday, and Wednesday, and on Thursday, they slaughtered it. For this reason, no liturgies are celebrated during these three days. The liturgy or the sacrifice on Maundy Thursday is the Lamb of God, Jesus Christ, who was slaughtered for the sins of the world.
This reasoning seems to ignore, or perhaps does not quite grasp the liturgical purpose of the rituals of the Maundy Thursday Liturgy, which I will attend to in due course.

The reason for this is that, during[13] the Passion Week, it is not permissible[14] to funeralize a deceased person inside the church or to raise incense. Instead, one of the parts of the Torah, whichever it is, is read over them.

Therefore, the fathers have arranged for the Funeral Prayers to be read on Palm Sunday[15] and to commemorate departed Christians. They would read either some, most or all the parts of the Funeral Prayers, time-permitting.

The *Manuscript of Uppsala*:

Then the priest reads the *Tobhs*[16] that came in the Pascha (book)[17], and the congregation says Lord Have Mercy in the short Pascha Tune twelve times; then the priest says the benediction and dismisses the congregation.

The *Manuscript of Paris* and the *Manuscript of Uppsala*:

And from the evening of that Sunday the stipulations of the Passion Week are implemented.[18]

---

[13] *Manuscript of Uppsala*: Written differently in the Arabic text.
[14] *Manuscript of Uppsala*: Written differently in the Arabic text.
[15] *Manuscript of Uppsala*: The Palm Feast.
[16] Tobhs is derived from the Coptic word Ⲧⲱⲃϩ (Tobh), meaning "Let us entreat."
[17] What is between parentheses has been added for clarification.
[18] The *Manuscript of Uppsala* adds the following text: We have abolished what the monks in the Shahran Monastery have decreed regarding the Procession of the Olive, as well as the order of Macarius Monastery in Upper Egypt, which consists of half a page and not more.
Refer to: Wadi the Franciscan, *op. cit.*, Volume 34, 259.

An Enquiry into the Author of the General Funeral Prayer

It is obvious from the previous account that the intended purpose for the General Funeral Prayer indicates that the Holy Paschal Week has not yet started.[19] In accordance with the old Coptic documents, we discover that the oldest known source known to date that speaks about this prayer goes back to the mid-eleventh century at the time of Pope Christodoulos (1047 – 1077), the 66th Patriarch of the Coptic Church. We read the following in his Canon No. 11:

> After the Liturgy on the Sunday of the Olive,[20] they read the Gospel and the Commemoration[21] of the Departed following the Pauline Epistle, known as the Epistle of the Departed.[22] Afterwards, they read the Absolution over all the people, because there should not be any absolution, commemoration or funeral during the Great Week[23] until the end of the Passover Feast.

---

[19] Cf. Dom Emmanuel Lanne, *op. cit.*, 287.
[20] "Sunday of the Olive" is the old name for Palm Sunday.
[21] In the manuscript No. 5997 at the British Museum (page 169 front), the word "" came as a translation of the Coptic word with the Greek origin Diptica (Diptikha).
Cf. Burmester, O.H.E. Khs, *The Canons of Christodoulos, Patriarch of Alexandria*, La Muséon t. XLV, 1932, 80, n.e.
[22] The account of this Service came in manuscript No. (5997 Add.), (page 16 back – 20 front). The Gospel Reading is from (John 5:19-30), the Pauline Epistle is from (1 Corinthians 15:1-27, 39-58).
Cf. O.E.E. Khs Burmester, *op. cit.*, Le Muséon t. XLV, 1932, 80, n.g.
[23] "Great Week" is the Holy Paschal Week, which concludes with the end of the prayers of Good Friday. Pope Christodoulos does not count Bright Saturday within the Paschal Week, as mentioned

It is very likely that Pope Christodoulos, who successfully discontinued the liturgical practice that went on for three centuries prior since the days of Pope Michael I (743 – 767) - that is reserving the Eucharist after the Palm Sunday Liturgy for communion on the days of the Holy Pascha - is the same person who instituted the General Funeral Prayer.

Aside from Canon No. 11, which was decreed by Pope Christodoulos, we have no earlier reference – so far – that even hints to this prayer or rite. This could be taken as evidence of his authoring this ritual. Furthermore, all the writings of Anba Severus Ibn Al-Muqaffa' (departed after 987 AD), the famous bishop who lived near the time of Pope Christodoulos, are devoid of any reference to this rite or prayer.

Therefore, after the time of Pope Christodoulos, that is after the eleventh century, we find writings by Ibn Sebā' and Ibn Kabar, amongst others, that the start of the Holy Paschal Week in the Coptic Church is Monday, and not Saturday (Lazarus Saturday) as mentioned by Anba Severus Ibn Al-Muqaffa' in the tenth century. Placing the General Funeral Prayer, as a preface to the Holy Paschal Week, right after the Palm Sunday Liturgy has removed Palm Sunday from the days of Holy Week.

---

in Canon No. 13 "And in the Liturgy of Bright Saturday, they read the Commemoration and the Absolution without greeting."

The Rite of the General Funeral Prayers according to the Manuscripts under Study

The *Manuscript of the Roman Quarter Typikon (15th century)* says the following:

> ... Then, they read the funeral of the dead: the men and women, the deacons and the priests, during the Distribution of the Divine Mysteries. Afterwards, they close the sanctuary veil[24] and the priest and deacons descend. The congregation says Ke τοy π̅ν̅ατι coy. The priest reads the three Minor Litanies, then the congregation says ϧεν ογμεθμηι[25] and the priests says Ce Ποc Ποc, ˙Νθοκ Ποc and Ⲫnhb Ποc.[26] The congregation says Lord Have Mercy in the Paschal Tune, and the priest concludes the Prayer by reciting the benediction and dismissing[27] the people.

The following is a summary of what the other manuscripts under study mention regarding the General Funeral Prayers. All manuscripts seem to agree on the liturgical components, that is, the Introduction to the Pauline, following by the Pauline Epistle. With respect to the Psalm Versicle, all manuscripts agree that it is read without hymn and then they respond in the

---

[24] That is, they close the door of the sanctuary.
[25] That is the Creed.
[26] That is the three absolutions.
[27] Written differently in the Arabic text.

Funeral Tune²⁸. Afterwards, they say the Introduction to the Gospel Ⲕⲉ ⳿ⲩⲡⲡⲉⲣ ⲧⲟⲩ (Ke Eperto), and they read the Gospel in the Paschal Tune and interpret it to the end of the rite of the funeral prayers. The manuscripts also agree that after the priest cleans the vessels, he descends from the sanctuary, shuts the sanctuary veil and stands before the door of the sanctuary to pray the three Litanies for the Peace, the Fathers, and the Assemblies.²⁹ Then, the Creed is recited, followed by the Litany of the Departed, the Lord's Prayer and the Absolution.

However, the manuscripts under study did not mention the Prophecy from the Book of Ezekiel (Ezekiel 37:1-14) that precedes the Pauline Epistle. This Prophecy does not exist in either the *Manuscript of St. Antony Lectionary (12ᵗʰ century)*, the *Manuscript of London Lectionary (12ᵗʰ century)*, or the *Manuscript of Paris Lectionary (14ᵗʰ century)*.

---

²⁸ As mentioned in the *Manuscript of Abba Shenoute Typikon (14ᵗʰ century)*.

²⁹ The manuscripts mention two expressions in this regard, the first is: "the priest stands before the veiled altar and prays the three litanies...," which could be found in the *Manuscript of Abba Shenoute Typikon (14ᵗʰ century)* and the *Manuscript of London Typikon*; while the second is "... descends from the altar, closes the veil, stands before the sanctuary door, and starts to pray the three litanies...," which could be found in the *Manuscript of the Hanging Church Typikon (16ᵗʰ century)*, the *Manuscript of Haret Zuweila Typikon (17ᵗʰ century)* and the *Manuscript of the Hanging Church Typikon*.

Now, let us turn to a more detailed exposition.

The Rite of the General Funeral Prayers according to the Church Order Manuscripts

In the following lines, I will include what the *Church Order Manuscript No. 118 (Rites) in Cairo Patriarchate for the year 1911* mentions, being an extension of the Church Order manuscripts, which date to the Middle Ages and are kept in the libraries of different churches and monasteries. Afterwards, I will turn to an explanation and commentary on the rite of the General Funeral Prayer and the different historical stages it underwent.

Under the title "The Order of the Palm Sunday Liturgy," the manuscript states the following[30]:

> ... Afterwards, they start reading the Funeral Prayer at the pulpit, as ought to be done. Then, they read the introduction to the Funeral Pauline Epistle as follows:

For the resurrection of the dead...	Ⲉⲑⲃⲉ ϯ`ⲁⲛⲁⲥⲧⲁⲥⲓⲥ `ⲛⲧⲉ ⲛⲓⲣⲉϥⲙⲱⲟⲩⲧ ...

> Then, they read the Psalm without hymn, and respond in the Funeral Tune. Afterwards, they say Ⲕⲉ `ⲩⲡⲡⲉⲣ ⲧⲟⲩ and read the Gospel in the Funeral Tune. They continue to read the Funeral Readings one after the other. At the end of the

---

[30] The same is also mentioned in the *Manuscript of Al-Baramūs Monastery 1514*.
Refer to: Samuel of Shibīn Al-Qanater, *op. cit.*, 61.

funeral and the distribution, the priest washes the vessels and his hands. He does not dismiss the congregation, but he closes the veil. Then, the celebrant priest goes down from the sanctuary and stands outside the door of the altar to pray the three Major Litanies for the Peace, the Fathers and the Assemblies, and the deacon responds. Afterwards, the people recite the Creed. Then, the priest prays the Litany of the Departed, and the deacon responds, while the congregation sits to have the Litany prayed over them, lest any of them would depart during the Holy Week. Then, the people say 'Our Father Who Art in Heaven' and the priest says: Cϵ Ⲡⲟⲥ Ⲡⲟⲥ and (also) Ⲛⲉⲟⲕ Ⲡⲟⲥ and the Absolution for the Son until the end. He, then, lifts the Cross and says Ⲫϯ ⲛⲁⲓ ⲛⲁⲛ in the Funeral Tune and the congregation responds with Lord Have Mercy in the Funeral Tune, alternating sides with each side saying it three times in the long tune and three in the short for a total of twelve times. Then, they say, 'Our Father,' and the priest recites the Paschal Benediction: 'Jesus Christ, our True God...'. They continue as customary, and the people are dismissed to their homes in peace.

Then, they return to the church at the Ninth Hour of the day, when the doors to the sanctuary are closed and a black or coloured cloth is placed on the sanctuary door. They also place the pulpit in the middle, covered in a black satin cloth or otherwise, and place the Paschal Book on it, and they start praying the Holy Pascha."

Explanation and Commentary on the Rite of the General Funeral Prayers

It is obvious from the previous account that, according to the Church Order manuscripts and the other manuscripts under study, the liturgical components that comprise the General Funeral Prayers are as follows:

1) The General Funeral Prayer begins after Psalm 150 is chanted without hymn, followed by "Ek Esmarout" in the Hosanna Tune. The sanctuary veil would be open during that time.

2) The introduction to the Pauline in the Funeral Tune Ⲉⲑⲃⲉ ⲧ̀ⲁⲛⲁⲥⲧⲁⲥⲓⲥ: "For the resurrection of the dead who have fallen asleep and reposed in the faith of Christ, O Lord repose all their souls."

3) The Pauline Epistle (1 Corinthians 15:1-27, 39-58) 31: "Christ died for our sins according to the Scriptures... But now Christ is risen from the dead, and has become the first fruits of those who have fallen asleep... For as in Adam all die, even so in Christ all shall be made alive. But each one in his own order."

4) The Psalm (Psalm 64): "Blessed is the man You choose, and cause to approach You, that he may dwell in Your courts. We shall be satisfied with the goodness of Your house. Holy is Your temple, wondrous in righteousness." According to the manuscripts, it is read without hymn and not in the Adrībī Tune.

---

[31] This Biblical reference is the same one mentioned in the *Manuscript of London Lectionary (12th century)*. However, some Holy Paschal Week Lectionaries have shortened the text.

The *Manuscript of London Lectionary (12th century)* includes the text for the Psalm as follows: "Blessed is he whom You choose and bring near to dwell in Your courts forever. Return, O my soul, to your rest, for the Lord has dealt bountifully with you. For You have delivered my soul from death, my eyes from tears, my feet from stumbling. I walk before the Lord in the land of the living."

5) The Introduction to the Gospel, Κε ˋγππερ τογ: "We beseech our Lord and God that we may be worthy to hear the Holy Gospel. In wisdom, let us listen to the Holy Gospel."

6) The Holy Gospel Reading (John 5:19-30): "For as the Father raises the dead and gives life to them, even so the Son gives life to whom He will… the hour is coming, and now is, when the dead will hear the voice of the Son of God; and those who hear will live."

The *Manuscript of London Lectionary (12th century)* includes after the Gospel Reading another one from Matthew about the woman who poured fragrant oil on His head in the house of Simon the Leper.

7) The three Major Litanies according to the Church Order manuscripts, or the three Minor Litanies according to the *Manuscript of the Roman Quarter Typikon (15th century)*.

8) Reciting the Creed.
9) The Litany of the Departed. However, this was not mentioned in the *Manuscript of the Roman Quarter Typikon (15th century)*.
10) The Lord's Prayer. It was not mentioned in the *Manuscript of the Roman Quarter Typikon (15th century)* but is implied when the manuscript mentions the Absolution prayers.
11) The Absolution prayers.
12) The Antiphonal "Kyrie Eleison" twelve times.
13) The Concluding Benediction.

The aforementioned elements are the same ones we read of by Pope Christodoulos (1047 - 1077) in the eleventh century, except for elements no. 6, 7, 9, 11 and 12. When Pope Christodoulos spoke of the "Commemoration of the Departed," he was referring to the Litany of the Departed which is prayed while raising incense, although he did not mention that explicitly.

In the thirteenth century, we read Ibn Sebā's account of these same liturgical components, save for a variation of element No. 11, where he says:

> The funeralizing of the all the people is performed wholly according to custom. It starts with raising incense and proceeding around the congregation with it, reciting the mournful funeral hymns as well as the Epistle in the Mournful Tune, which starts with: 'Moreover, brethren, I

declare to you the gospel which I preached to you, which also you received...', followed by the Psalm, the Gospel Reading, and the Absolution as usual. After the Absolution according to custom, they say Lord Have Mercy 100 times. Afterwards, the Homily is read to the congregation, and the Pascha begins from the Eleventh Hour of the Sunday.[32]

Furthermore, Ibn Kabar (1324 AD) also refers to these general liturgical components, saying:

> ... And when the Liturgy is over and they have started to commune, they do not chant Psalm 150, but start reciting the Funeral Prayer, one reading after the other, starting with the Pauline Epistle, the Psalm, and the Gospel of funeralizing the departed, until they finish Communion to occupy the congregation with the readings until the end of the distribution.[33]

The recent Typika include a Prophecy from the Book of Ezekiel (37:1-14) that is to be read before the Pauline Epistle. In this Prophecy, the Lord says:

> Behold, O My people, I will open your graves and cause you to come up from your graves... I will put My Spirit in you, and you shall live... I, the Lord, have spoken it and performed it.

---

[32] Yoḥanna Ibn Zakaria Ibn Sebā', *op. cit.*, 312-324.
[33] Shams al-Ri'āsa Abū al-Barakāt Ibn Kabar, *The Lamp of Darkness and the Clarification of the Service* (*Miṣbāḥ al-ẓulma wa 'īḍāḥ al-khidma*), Manuscript No. 203 (Arabic), National Library in Paris, Section 18.

Let us all stand during the General Funeral Prayers with bowed heads as the dry bones because of our many transgressions, so that we may hear the word of the Lord in faith, however simple, to open a way for it into our hearts. Let the word of the Lord enter our inner parts, discerning the thoughts of our hearts and our intentions, purify and wash our consciences and lives, for we are standing here dead in our iniquities and sins.

It is important to note here that, amongst twenty different Holy Paschal Week Lectionary manuscripts scattered in the libraries around the world and examined by O.H.E. Burmester,[34] one manuscript was found in the Catholic Institute of Paris[35], which includes the following sentence in its beginning: "On Palm Sunday, they read this Prophecy from Isaiah during the Distribution." After this title, the manuscript includes the text of the Prophecy of Isaiah from (Isaiah 40:9-31).[36]

Sprinkling the Water at the End of the General Funeral Prayers

The sprinkling of water at the end of the Palm Sunday Liturgy and the General Funeral Prayers is for the congregation and not for the palms, which is the

---

[34] *PO*, t. 24, fasc. 2, 176.
[35] Ms Copte 6 (Paris: Institut Catholique de Paris).
[36] Oswald H.E. KHS-Burmester, *The Turuhat of the Coptic Church*, op. cit., 91.

standard ritual that follows the end of every Liturgy. There is no relation between this sprinkling of water and the prayers of the General Funeral, which nowadays is performed at the end of the Liturgy of this great day.

This water is for dismissing the people as is usual in every Liturgy. It is not the funeral water as it is sometimes called. There are no prayers on the water during the Funeral prayers, nor is there water to be sprinkled on the people. Instead, incense is raised as in any other funeral prayer prayed over any of the departed during the year. The only difference is that it is a funeral prayer over the living. Nowhere in the utterance of the entire Funeral Prayer is there a mention of the word "water," and there is no sanctification of water or any other liturgical ritual concerning the water.

Perhaps the confusion of the Funeral Prayer and the use of water on this day arose due to the font that some churches place in the sanctuary to attend the Divine Liturgy on this day, and thus also the General Funeral Prayer that follows. However, the use of this font has its origins in the ancient Hebrew Rite of the Feast of Tabernacles, where the priest brings water in a golden jar from the Pool of Siloam and carries it to the altar to pour it there. This ritual is a symbol of the events of Palm Sunday, and not the Funeral Prayers.[37]

---

[37] Fr Matthew the Poor mentions in the first part of his book "Exegesis into the Gospel of St. John" (p. 726), edition of the year

Many people seem to think that the sprinkling of water at the end of the Funeral Prayers is to bless the palms. This matter needs to be entirely remediated and brought to people's attention. It is important to note here that the Eastern Churches, except the Maronite Church which follows the Latin Rite, do not know a ritual for blessing the palms.[38] On the other hand, the Western Latin Tradition is the only one that includes a ritual for blessing the palms the people carry on this day. In the early days it was a long ritual but has been recently abridged.

1990, the following: "Some priests mistakenly consecrate it (that is the palm branches) with the water of the Lakkan of the Departed, which the priests undertake lest anyone would depart during the Passion Week, during which it is not permissible to perform any prayers on the departed but only sprinkle them with the water of the Lakkan of the Departed." This matter was not mentioned in any of the old liturgical references or the Church Order manuscripts that continued to be written from generation to generation until the beginning of the twentieth century. It is important to note here that since 1987, a font of water is placed with two candles around it before starting the General Funeral Prayers, which are performed at 3 o'clock in the afternoon in the monastery of St. Macarius. Then, it is taken away at the end of the General Funeral Prayers without performing any liturgical prayers on it. I do not know the reason for this practice!

[38] What appeared in the book "The Desire of the Souls in the Order of the Rites" (p. 93) that the consecration of the palms is performed in the Matins Raising of Incense during the Procession of the Twelve Gospels instead of after the General Funeral is not true. I do know who said that, for this is an odd matter that is not supported by any liturgical references, old or new!

As for the Byzantine Church, it has specific prayers that are prayed on the palms on this feast. Since the year 397 AD, the blessing of the palms on this day has been practiced in all the Mesopotamian Churches

Bibliography

Primary Sources

Abu Almakarem. *The History of the Churches and Monasteries in the Twelfth Century*, Volume 2.

All manuscripts in *Index of Manuscripts used in this Study*

Basset, René. *Le synaxaire arabe Jacobite: (rédaction copte). IV, Les mois de barmahat, barmoudah, et bachons*. Dans *Patrologia Orientalis (PO)*, t. XVI, fasc. 2, Paris, 1922.

Burmester, O.H.E. Khs. *Le lectionaire copte de la semaine sainte*. Dans *Patrologia Orientalis (PO)* 24, fas.2, Paris, 1933.

Burmester, O.H.E. Khs. *The Canons of Christodulos, Patriarch of Alexandria*. Dans *Le Muséon* t. XLV, 1932.

Burmester, O.H.E. Khs. *The Homilies and Exhortation of the Holy Week*. Dans *Le Muséon* 45, 1932.

Burmester, O.H.E. Khs. *The Turuhat of the Coptic Church*. OCP, Volume 3, 1937.

Burmester, O.H.E. Khs. *The Two Services of the Coptic Church Attributed to Peter, Bishop of Behnasa*.

Clavis Patrum Graecorum (CPG). Edited by Maurice Geerard, Volume 1. Brepols-Turnhout, 1983.

Eusebius of Caeserea. *Ecclesiastical History*. Translated by Arthur Cushman McGiffert. From Nicene and Post-Nicene Fathers, Second Series, Vol. 1. Edited by Philip Schaff and Henry Wace. Buffalo, NY: Christian Literature Publishing Co., 1890. Revised and edited for New Advent by Kevin Knight, 5 August 2021, <http://www.newadvent.org/fathers/2501.htm>.

John Chrysostom. *On Genesis*. Translated by Robert C. Hill, CUA Press Fathers of the Church Patristic Series 82. Washington, D.C.: The Catholic University of America Press, 1990.

Severus Ibn Al-Muqaffa' of Al-Ashmūnīn. *History of the Holy Church*, Vol. 2. Edited by Yassā 'abd Al-Masīḥ, Aziz Soriel 'ateya and Oswald H.E. KHS-Burmester. Cairo: Publications de la Société d'Archéologie Copte, 1959.

Severus Ibn Al-Muqaffa' of Al-Ashmūnīn. *The Precious Pearls in Explaining the Faith*. Tosson, Shubra: Archangel Michael Church, 1987.

Shams al-Riʾāsa Abū al-Barakāt Ibn Kabar. *The Lamp of Darkness and the Clarification of the Service* (*Miṣbāḥ al-ẓulma wa 'īḍāḥ al-khidma*). Manuscript No. 203 (Arabic), National Library in Paris. Translated by Samir Khalil. Cairo: al-Karouz Library, 1971.

Sozomen. *Ecclesiastical History*. Translated by Chester D. Hartranft. From Nicene and Post-Nicene Fathers, Second Series, Vol. 2. Edited by Philip Schaff and Henry Wace. Buffalo, NY: Christian Literature Publishing Co., 1890. Revised and edited for New Advent by Kevin Knight, 5 August 2021, <http://www.newadvent.org/fathers/2602.htm>.

Yoḥanna Ibn Zakaria Ibn Sebā'. *Book of the Precious Jewel in Church Sciences (Ketāb al-Jawhara al-Nafīsa Fī 'Oloum al-Kanīsa)*. Verified and translated to Latin by Father Victor Mansour Mestarīḥ the Franciscan. Cairo: The Franciscan Center for Eastern Christian Studies, 1966.

Secondary Sources

Abd Al-Masih, Yassa. *Doxologies in the Coptic Church*. Dans *BSAC*, t. IV, 1938.

Baumstark, Anton. *Comparative Liturgy*. English Edition By F.L. Cross, London, 1958.

Budge, E.A. Wallis. *Coptic Homilies in the Dialect of Upper Egypt*. London, British Museum, 1910.

Burmester, O.H.E. Khs. *The Egyptian or Coptic Church, A Detailed Description of her Liturgical Services and the Rites and Ceremonies Observed in the Administration of her sacraments*. BSAC, Textes et Documents, X, Le Caire, 1967.

Burmester, O.H.E. Khs. "The Greek Kirugmata, Versicles and Responses, and Hymns in the Coptic Liturgy." *Orientalia Christiana Periodica II*, 3-4, 1936.

Cross, F.L. & Livingstone, E.A. *The Oxford Dictionary of The Christian Church (ODCC)*. 2nd edition, 1988.

Drescher, John. *The Earliest Biblical Concordances. BSAC* Copte 15, 1958-1960.

Emmanuel Lanne, Dom. *Textes et rites de la liturgie pascale dans l'ancienne église Copte*. Dans *L'Orient Syrien*, 6, 1961.

Kamel, Morad. *The Coptic Era in the History of the Egyptian Civilization*. Cairo, 1963.

Lantschoot, A. van. *Le Ms. Vatic. Copte 44 et le livre de Chrême (ms. Paris arabe 100)*. Dans *Le Muséon*, t. XLV, Cahiers 3-4, Louvain, 1932.

Louis Villecourt, Dom, O.S.B. *Le livre du chrême (ms. Paris arabe 100)*. *Le Muséon*, t. XLI, 1928.

Louis Villecourt, Dom, O.S.B. *Les observances liturgiques et la discipline du jeûne dans l'église Copte*. *Le Muséon*, 37, 1924.

Louis Villecourt, Dom, O.S.B. avec le concours de Mgr. Eugène Tisserant, M. Gaston Wiet, *Livre de la lampe des ténèbres et de l'exposition (Lumineuse) du service (de l'église)*. Dans *Patrologia Orientalis (PO)*, tome XX, fascicule 4, N. 99, Turnhout/Belgique, 1974.

Menards, Otto. *The Itinerary of the Holy Family in Egypt*, dans *Collectanea*, No. 7.

Our Liturgical Life, Liturgical Studies, 1st year. Lebanon, 1989-1990.

Our Liturgical Life, Liturgical Studies, 2nd year. No. 16 Azar. Lebanon, 1991.

Queck, Hans. *Untersuchungen zum koptischen stundengebet*. Louvain, 1970.

Rizk, Majid Ṣ. Journal of New Vine, 2008.

Samuel of Shibīn Al-Qanater. *The Church Order as per the Patriarchate manuscripts in Cairo and Alexandria and the manuscripts of the monasteries and churches*, Volume 3. Cairo, 2000.

Studia Orientalia Christiana, Collectanea 34, Studia – Documenta. The Franciscan Center of Christian Oriental Studies, Cairo - Jerusalem, 2001.

The Biblical Knowledge Society, Volume 1.

The Desire of the Souls in the Order of the Rites. Coptic Orthodox Church Cantors Association, 1986.

The New Oxford Annotated Bible.

Theological Dictionary of the New Testament, Volume IX.

Viaud, Gérard. *La procession des deux fêtes de la croix et du dimanche des rameaux dans l'église Copte.* Dans BSAC, 19, 1970.

Wadi the Franciscan, *Christian Oriental Studies,* Volume 34. Cairo – Jerusalem: The Franciscan Center of Christian Oriental Studies, 2001.

Youssef, Youhanna N. *Procession of The Cross and The Palm Sunday According to A Manuscript from Saint Macarius. BSAC,* t. XLVI, 2007.

Made in the USA
Middletown, DE
27 September 2023